PRAISE FOR LAURE-ANNE BOSSELAAR

For *The Hour Between Dog & Wolf*

Laure-Anne Bosselaar understands the complexities and the endless contradictions of our contemporary human predicament. Hers is an authentic poetic voice, one serious enough to be heard at the end of this long and brutal century. She writes wise poems about memory, poems whose art lies in their ability to make these memories ours too. What more could any one of us ask of poetry?

— Charles Simic

For *Small Gods of Grief*

With a depth and a musicality that is stunning, *Small Gods of Grief* sings a path from sorrow to reverence. Here is poetry for the breath taking back the beauty that should have been. We are, all of us, redeemed by these poems.

— Claudia Rankine

I love Laure-Anne Bosselaar's poems because they remind me of why I love poetry: because it can make me feel so alive it doesn't matter that death is all around. *Small Gods of Grief* does that. It affirms, it affirms.

— Thomas Lux

With a paradoxical joining of muscle and delicacy Laure-Anne Bosselaar crafts poems of great intelligence, music and spirit. *Small Gods of Grief* is powerful work in which she displays all the poet's gifts. I returned to these poems again and again.

— Stephen Dobyns

Here are poems from the inside, sung by an outsider whose need to be part of that which is not evil allows her to see herself and us in the world with enormous heart and tentative hope. Laure-Anne Bosselaar has written a large book whose sweep pushes us aside, pushes us under, pushes us forward.

— Martha Rhodes

For *A New Hunger*

"There's a time in the life of a poet as a maker of poems, if she or he is going to become more than just good, when the voice of one's second self fully emerges, distilling and orchestrating the poet's concerns, while simultaneously infusing them with an inner melody — a music that reaches and satisfies both ear and mind. This is to say that Laure-Anne Bosselaar, with her wonderful third book, *A New Hunger*, has become more than just good. It's an occasion to mark and to celebrate. Jacques Maritain says that he'd like poetry "…to turn self-awareness into a superior sort of simplicity," and this is what, page after page, Bosselaar does. From the long poem that begins the collection and the ambitious sonnet sequence that follows it, to almost any of the shorter lyrics, she shows a masterful control of pacing and tone. And all of the poems feel necessary, embodied. She's written a book of urgent meditations, which places her already good work on a new level. I love what she's done.

— Stephen Dunn

For *These Many Rooms*

These Many Rooms is a sequence of elegies that build to an almost unbearable depth of feeling. They do this not by the rending of clothing or the tearing of hair, but by a subtle, understated study of self as the days and then years pass after the death of a husband. Brimming with grief, the poems alternately shimmer and darken, exploring not only one person's unique experience, but the nature of grieving itself. In a language that's simultaneously inventive and plainspoken, Bosselaar charges the ordinary world with the electricity of memory and emotion, so that we feel the missing person's presence everywhere. These many rooms is moving, profound, and unforgettable, not the least because it shows us how beauty can be both a solace and a wound. This is a book I'll return to again and again.

— Chase Twichell

Laure-Anne Bosselaar's luminous poems mourn the loss of her dear beloved even as they become a testament to the possibility of profound, abiding friendship and love. With compassionate attention, she observes herself in these rooms of life and of grief. Her attention is patient, humble, courageous, and leaves us with a stunningly clear, unadorned trace of a tender history. Inside of her words are windows, darkness and light — a book, a shared life "alive with its own clarity." Such texts feel ancient, ongoing. I am forever deepened (taught to listen). Forever moved.

— Aracelis Girmay

With language both lush and unflinching, Laure-Anne Bosselaar's new collection allows us a long look at what lost love means in the most beautiful and poignant sense of those words. How do we — how can we — make a way through the vast, invisible territory that stretches before each of us when death claims someone for whom our hearts had awakened gloriously and completely? Such grief demands that we feel too much; we find ourselves pressed into a silence that even our closest companions hesitate to engage. In *These Many Rooms*, Laure-Anne Bosselaar breaks open this silence, writing frankly and with sublime grace on this difficult walk. As she chronicles life after the sudden passing of her husband, the wonderful poet Kurt Brown, we are offered an intricately detailed map of that half-lit wilderness each person must enter when confronted by overwhelming loss.

— Tim Seibles

LATELY

New & Selected Poems

by
Laure-Anne Bosselaar

SUNGOLD EDITIONS • SANTA BARBARA
2024

www.laureanne.net

Published by Sungold Editions

Cover art is "Venetian Mooring" by Emily Mason
Author photo by Abram Katz

Hardcover ISBN-13: 979-8-9867290-7-7
Paperback ISBN-13: 979-8-9867290-6-0

For Tibo

CONTENTS

TWO LONGER POEMS

FOREWORD

THE WORLDS IN THIS WORLD

Doors were left open in heaven again:
drafts wheeze, clouds wrap their ripped
pages around roofs and trees. Like wet
flags, shutters flap and fold. Even light
is blown out of town, its last angles caught
in sopped newspaper wings and billowing
plastic — all this in one American street.

Elsewhere, somewhere, a tide recedes,
incense is lit, an infant sucks from a nipple,
a grenade shrieks, a man buys his first cane.
Think of it: the worlds in this world.

Yesterday, while a Chinese woman took
hours to sew seven silk stitches into
a tapestry started generations ago, guards
took only seconds to mop up a cannibal's
brain from the floor of a Wisconsin jail,
while the man who bashed the killer's head
found no place to hide, and sat sobbing
for his mother in a shower stall —
the worlds in this world.

Or say, one year — say in 1916 —while
my grandfather, a prisoner of war in Holland,
sewed perfect, eighteen-buttoned booties
for his wife with the skin of a dead dog found
in a trench, shrapnel slit Apollinaire's skull,
Jesuits brandished crucifixes in Ouagadougou,
and the Parthenon was already in ruins.

That year, thousands and thousands of Jews
from the Holocaust were already — were still —
busy living their lives, while gnawed by self-
doubt, Rilke couldn't write a line for weeks
in Vienna's Viktorgasse, and fishermen drowned
off Finnish coasts, and lovers kissed for the very
first time, while in Kashmir an old woman
fell asleep, her cheek on her good husband's belly.

And all along that year the winds kept blowing
as they do today, above oceans and steeples,
and this one speck of dust was lifted from
somewhere to land exactly here, on my desk,
and will lift again — into the worlds in this world.

Say now, at this instant: one thornless rose
opens in a blue jar above that speck, but you —
reading this — know nothing of how it came
to flower here, and I nothing of who bred it,
or where, nothing of my son and daughter's
fate, or of what grows in your garden or behind
the walls of your chest? Tell me, is it longing?
Fear? Will it matter?

Listen to that wind, listen to it ranting
The doors of heaven never close, that's the Curse,
that's the Miracle.

from
LATELY

PARENTAGE

Mine is not from the morass of Flanders'
marshes, although their hues ink my eyes.

Not from a mother: her head spun, always,
away.

Nor from convent walls or kisses I hid —
head bowed — inside my childhood palms
to quiet longing. Such longing.

But from a Flemish farmer, once,
who held my face in both hands to kiss
my brow for no more than a second —

that brief — but with such will & tenderness
that I can now lift my head far back,
to read the clouds.

I'm from the ocean's melancholy, dragging
its anchors back & forth, never quiet, never
still, its waves so restless

they can't mirror the moon. From those tides,
those ebbings.

From two wedding bands on my finger,
from them too —

& from every book I ever held: my shelved
provenance, language womb, & sail.

ODE TO THE SCHORREN

& their skin-thin silt the Scheldt ground
down from rocks, slopes & swamps —
that rainy-day-gray mud, a satin muck
that slips through fingers & escapes toward
the insatiable North Sea.

Neptune was born there a farmer told me,
in that estuary where the sky is so low,
you can sip it from your lips.

No horizon, not a farm or field or path —
only unbound marshes moored under
the constant giggle of cloud-ghosting gulls.

It's this sludge, marsh-soaked, that the winds
whistle to & wrinkle — braiding pickleweed
& widgeon grass — where cat-sized muskrats
shriek & pull bitterns down into the sludge
by the feet.

Everything there is sopped with everything:
light with silt, silt with clouds, clouds with rain
& sloughs with rot & slime.

But in the Spring, when griseous clouds swell
high in the air, sun-shafts dive, sudden & brilliant,
deep into the gullies' throats, & if you wait long
enough, right there:

out of the vaguely swaying sedge, you'll hear it:
the soar of the marsh warbler's song —
& it's then that you'll press both hands to your heart.
Both hands to your heart.

FIRST MORNING OF THE NEW YEAR

It is early. A bird flies deep into the sky —
into that large silence — the sun so new
it weaves hair-thin rays through the mist
& weeds. Then a first crow caw, & another.
I'm all willing attention, as I was yesterday,
walking along the ocean's wrack line,
while the waves swallowed the year's last
light, then shatter it into fireworks of droplets,
before they too crashed, dying on the sand
& rocks. But this whisper of a morning is
all mystery still — some ferns & tree
my only company, & I ask nothing of them
but to give me the time to breathe in this hour,
and the time for it to take me where it will.

MONTHS INTO THE PANDEMIC

The wait for night's end is almost over.
Although it isn't a wait, really, more like
an abeyance — night's last breaths before
the curtains are aflame with light.

I lie very still, breathing in the same air
as this dawning & its clouds, barely
visible, but soon red-bellied like the finch
as it throws back its head to sing to them.

Such abandon around me: dawn to day,
silence to song, clouds to sky, as night
folds on itself like origami, & the moon
yields to transparency.

Later, from under the tree, I'll look up
at that sky, clouds & morning-blue fused
together by a kintsugi of branches.

May I be here, still, at day's end. May we lean
a while against each other again, that tree & I.
Against each other & into the darker hours too.

COMPLAINT ABOUT MISSING FRIENDS
A YEAR INTO THE PANDEMIC

No one near to see or hear me but the dog,
who sighs when I say serious things & I'm dead
serious when I tell her how her gray muzzle
is softer than Samarkand silk.

No one to tell I just read that on hot August
nights, Verlaine threw pail after pail after
cold water pail on the gravel under Rimbaud's
windows, to cool the air as he slept.

No one to side-step with me to some silly tune —
as the dog's tail wags out of rhythm — or listen
to my Flemish song about spring coming soon
& the *Phallus Impudicus* being almost in bloom.

To see me kneel by the rosemary, breathing in
its oily green before night comes flitting into
the yard & the skunks & raccoons join in to feast
on such fresh darkness.

No friends to be here with me & all this & wave,
fondly, as they leave the garden, the dog, the evening
& me. But leaving behind that lilt in their voices —
goodnight, goodnight.

LATE AFTERNOON STROLL ON THE CLIFFS

As usual, Death sweetly slips her arm in mine —
& we take a deep breath from the eucalyptus breeze.
We both worked honestly at our jobs: all day Death
destroyed traffic with wailing ambulances while I killed
hours & lines on eight-&-a-half by eleven inch pages.
We're fast friends by now, Death much older of course,
but there's no hierarchy between us: we're both taking
a break from it all, glad to watch waves collapse on rocks
& pelicans dive-bomb fish. I try to be sensitive to Death's
guilt: that whole pandemic disaster she can no longer
control. She'll soon betray me too — like she will you.
I know. But today the gulls are silver angels etching
great cursive blessings in a perfect sky — so Death & I
make believe we believe that, & amble on.

WHEN THE BED IS MADE

I love that nameless gesture, that large,
broad sweep: a final, flat-palmed smoothing
of the covers — an almost instinctive stroke
to the bed before leaving the room. How
I have done it — as you have — year after year.
How mothers, lovers, husbands, nurses,
backs aching, bent over beds for that last
swift tidying. Over the night cries, grabs,
terrors & sweats. Hidden, the love-stained
sheets, or the much too impeccable ones.
Hushed the whispers, confidences, & all
the given, taken, or turned-away from kisses.
And so we leave the rooms, the made beds.
Nights tucked beneath their smooth surface.

EARLY MORNING CONSIDERATIONS
AFTER A NIGHT OF RAIN

There you are, first light freckling the curtains
with dawn while the jay insists: *It's six. Six!*
It's six — as if I don't know that.

Good morning, welcome, new Thursday. I arc
the blankets away. The dog sheds gladness all
around me as war news shrapnels out of NPR.

Outside, everything is still gleam & green after
the first rain in months, & *petrichor* — a word some
poets sequin into their pastorals — left with the wind.

Petrichor! I imagine a starched table & gold candles
as erect-pinkie'd connoisseurs sniff a Zin & a guest
highbrows: *I adore me a good petrichor.*

It's not in my vocabulary of choice. Give me
glad-deep-earth-breath instead, & for rain try
window-tickler, soak-notes, or *gutter-mutterers*

I could go on & on, & I do, actually — aloud,
& alone. So I'll stop here, but not before
telling you what word makes me want to curtsey

to the heavens & aubade each dawn: it's *sempiternal.*
Sem-pi-ter-nal. May it be *the* final word, so that
when the last fire or virus, bombed-down night

or hate-cloaked day are done being done, *sempiternal* —
charred perhaps, soaked or scarred — will clear its throat,
shoot a root, try a trill, jump-start a new heart, & reign.

KITE AT DAYBREAK ON THE CLIFF'S EDGE

At first, I think it's a plastic bag, ripped to ribbons
& billowing wild inside a wild wind. But when it
drops toward the beach I see the man, ancient,
ragged. He pulls a spool to his heart, turns, faces
the cliff & unwinds the string to let his kite rise
up again, but toward me this time. It sways, soars
high into the light-soaked sky as the day opens
to the sun. But the winds shift & lift the kite higher
& toward the ocean. The man tugs at the spool,
pulls, pulls back hard as he rewinds the string.
The kite resists, fights back, pulls madly toward
the horizon, but the string will not break, so —
it lets go, falls, slowly, toward the sands to lie
down, terribly still, at the feet of its maker.

GODWIT BEACH

How appeased they are today, those waves —
limpid, crowning shoulder-to-shoulder —
old lovers come to linger on these sands,
companions of furious storms and Pacific languor.

Limpid, crowning shoulder-to-shoulder,
like us, love, they remind me of us those tides:
companions of furious storms and Pacific languor,
we walked a while along these sandstone cliffs.

Like us, love, they remind me of us, those tides.
Remember? It was late in the afternoon,
we walked a while along these sandstone cliffs,
under the silver ghosts of eucalyptus trees.

Remember? It was late in the afternoon
we said: *yes, yes, this is where we belong, isn't it:*
under the silver ghosts of eucalyptus trees,
as the day blushes so frankly there, way in the west.

We said: *yes, yes, this is where we belong, isn't it?*
Old lovers come to linger on these sands,
as the day blushes so frankly there, way in the west.
How appeased they are today, those waves.

WALKING HOME FROM THE STORE

The dog won't even pull at the leash anymore:
we're both tired from the uphill hike. The day
runs out of light behind an old sycamore. From
neighbor's homes the kitchen jingles I love:
cymbals of silverware drawers, a lid's tap dance
on a pan. Silhouettes shift against TV flickers.
The dog & I are the only ones left in the street
now, & it comes to me that we could be a perfect
image in a Tranströmer poem: an old widow
& her black dog in a dusk-dark street. But just
as we enter our house, the new moon shines her
bright, thin grin through the kitchen's open window,
& the mockingbird finally breaks into one of his
delirious nocturnes — pure & zealous & breathless.

SOMETIMES,

        when a branch pulls at my sleeve
like a child's tug, or the fog, reticent & thick, lifts,
& strands of it still hang like spun sugar on branches
& twigs, or when a phoebe trills in the olive tree,
        I believe such luck is meant only
for me. Does this happen to you? Do you believe that,
at times, a moment actually chooses you to remember it
entirely & tell about it — so that it may live again?

CONJUGATION

Tenth anniversary of his death,
and a few friends call still —

We loved him. He was a kind man.
We miss him. "*Loved*" & "*was*"

gone with him into the past tense,
yet "*miss*" is still so very much

in the present. Good friends:
they bring him back to me with

that missing. But I don't mention
this. One fears sentimentality.

Nor do I tell them how I wondered
at his intricate syntax when he spoke

to the cat. Or how often I'd stop
being busy, to listen to him being

so noisily alive. I was going
to tell him that.

EVENING

Gone. Another day gone. Its chest-
shredding tragedies or frivolous whims equally
scavenged by dusk. Soon the wind will come rest
in the knotty trellis of my tree.

But in the west, sudden, the sun's last blades
pierce the dusk & stain the clouds' vanishing,
so that, for an instant, the whole sky is ablaze
with dying — its own radiant dying —

then twilight dulls it all. I'll gladly give in
to what it will bring: the good book I'll return to,
the possum's wobble in the yard, the moon's dream-
catcher as it whisps in & out of the mist — it too

soon invisible under the weary lids of night.

BRIEF

It happens so often: there — somewhere
in a line, waiting room or store — I see you,

& it's something about your work-wrecked
hands, cow-lick, the perfect curl of your lips,

or grief nearly collapsing your face,
that make me quietly smile at you or nod

as I take you in — nameless companion
in this crammed commute of a life —

& whether you lower your eyes or smile
back, I now carry you along with me,

& remember you some day as I walk
the dog or drive to the mall —

amazed & glad to have you close again,
albeit for the smallest moment.

INVITATION

Awkward crumb-of-a-cloud, little orphan,
forlorn trawl over the neighbor's roof,

you shapeless left-over nimbostratus —
don't be gone, so much is already torn,

already worn. Stay: I see you. I notice.
Don't fade away like some frayed regret,

don't cast over or conk out: all the clouds
do that, you weary wilt of a haze. Come

here. Shun the dusk, show off those ambers
& pinks as the sun dies again on the other

side of town. But if you must let go, come
pebble at my window, pour your heart out

here, soak the sorrel by the tree. It's a good
place to rain over. A good place to be.

AT THE END OF THE BREAKWATER

The pelicans begin their morning journey —
so low into the waves' furrows that there's only
a feather of air between the water & their gullets.
Mist unbraids its ribbons from the palm fronds.
The tide sways the kelp back & forth.

Less than half a mile away, commuters rush past
on the highway, their shush so like the swash waves
as they die on the sands. Let the day open so wholly
to light. Let me stand here, very still, my journey
almost over. Let the ocean silver all round me.

TONIGHT'S DINNER COMPANIONS

As dinner simmers on the stove, I set
a place at the table for

you, thin & dog-eared book I never tire
of dog-earing again,

& you, wind-whirr coming in to flutter
the book's pages too,

& you, photo of a stout Flemish farmer
brandishing seven dead muskrats,

& you, memory of a Brussels attic: my hand
over my first lover's hand on my heart — weighing,

& you, good friend, gone, whose lines I often say
aloud against the ocean's incessant *shush*,

& you, my love's baseball cap, the one he kept
losing & is now on a shelf, never to be lost again,

& you, reader, to whom I have been writing
most of my life — here: this place is for you.

from
THE HOUR BETWEEN DOG
AND WOLF

LITTLE SISTERS OF LOVE AND MISERY

May Field Trip to Ostend

When the slaughterhouse smoke was no longer blown
inland by the wind, but North, to the sea, and the lapwings
blabbered behind the chapel; when the refectory tables

were freckled with strawberries, and it was no longer dark
at Matins' *Ite Missa Est*, when punishment switched
from praying to weeding the rose garden,

and novices bleached their aprons in the sun — Judith, Marie
and I started counting the days till the first Sunday in May.
That morning, Sister Serena distributed our summer uniforms,

Mother Superior rounded up every one for the Field Trip to Ostend,
and Sister Kelleen tapped the shoulders of three girls
who were to stay behind to help her chafe the chapel floor.

For the last four years it had been us: we never broke
the silence about the only time she broke hers, never spoke —
even among each other — about what happened those nights,

or wondered why. To this day, I still can't explain. But this
I know: a kind pain breaks in me when I see broken glass,
or wine spilled. A kind pain. We all have a few.

Sister Kelleen

She was pale, thin, young, tall. Because she was Irish and barely
spoke Flemish, she couldn't teach, and was given the chapel to keep.
It was said she tended to it in the middle of the night,

walking through the rose-garden as if in daylight, choosing
the lushest rose for St. Bosco. Winters, she folded a different
colored handkerchief at his feet every day, though

no one saw her do it. Or smile, or lift her eyes. But in May,
on Field Trip Day, Sister Kelleen woke from her torpor. It started
with her foot, at breakfast, although with the refectory

bustling with lunch-packing and strawberry eating, I think
no one noticed but me. Like a bird caught in a net, her foot
fluttered, quivered, then jerked under the swart hem of her habit.

The motion crept to her knees, hips, her crucifix swayed, not
sideways but beating her chest. Her hands escaped
from the black tunnels of her sleeves, one stilling the crucifix,

the other her knees. Eyes afire, she watched the school
escape in the sun-drunk street in uniformed rows of three.
Voices stopped echoing from the nunnery:

the school was empty but for Judith, Marie, Sister Kelleen
and me. *Mes petites soeurs d'amour et de misère,*
she whispered once: *my little sisters of love and misery...*

Glass-Shard Night

We followed her, silently, through empty corridors,
dank pantry stairs, through coal and furnace rooms,
to the tiny mass-wine cellar. Empty bottles were piled

on the dirt floor, the full ones — like stiff rows of nuns —
were locked behind the grated doors of an oak cupboard.
Sister Kelleen shut the cellar door, handed us each

a pair of black cotton gloves: Shards, girls, we need good
sharp shards, opened the cupboard, snatched a bottle,
pulled out the cork, & took long gulps — and we knew

what to do: kneel by the empty bottle pile, slip on the gloves,
grab a bottle by its neck, and wait for the signal. It never took long:
with a wail, her half-empty bottle split the air over our heads

and shattered against the wall. The cellar shook with her cry, the crash
of glass on bricks. It was our turn. We hurled our empty bottles.
From behind us — More!— she threw hers, sopping us with claret,

and we screamed and shrieked, bumped into each other,
as she drank and drank, and bottles shattered — More! More! —
until a winter's worth of masses lay smashed on the cellar floor.

Hair & faces soaked with wine, we wrapped our knees
with newspaper and knelt by the pile. We knew better than
to look: every breath a sob now, Sister Kelleen drank,

drank and wept, while, heads bowed, we filled our skirts
with shards, large enough to have a good grip on them, sharp
enough to scrape the chapel floor.

Night Song

A burning candle in one hand, wine bottle in the other, she lit
every votive in the chapel. On the altar steps, on a blue kitchen
towel, her offering to us: a jug of milk, a rock of black chocolate,

a loaf of brown bread. Next to it, we placed our alms to her: a green,
gleaming heap of shards. We sat in a circle on the floor. We ate.
She drank. Then: Now, she ordered, Now — and started singing:

Kelleen, Kelleen drunk, tore
the cornet from her head, rolled black knitted
stockings down her freckled legs,

tied her habit's hem to her waist — and sang.
Loud and proud, she sang. And all night,
to the sway of her songs,

we scraped and chafed, shard in fist, back and forth,
back and forth, and planed the chapel floor's
hard knotted boards.

Kelleen beside us, singing of whalers and sailors
and far-away shores, of foghorns and luggers,
and brothels and whores.

And the more she sang,
the finer we scraped,
as golden wood curls twirled.

Crucifixion Dawn

And every year, at the hour the lapwings woke
behind the chapel and night folded like a handkerchief
at St. Bosco's feet, she walked to the altar, faced the crucifix,

prayed *Pie Jesu, tantus labor non sit cassus,* turned around,
and spat on the floor. Bowing our heads again, we went
to her. She held our heads to her belly, blessed us —

a cross thumbed on our foreheads and lips, whispering:
Go. Pray for me. Pray. Chased into silence, we stepped
across the impeccable floor, closed the chapel door,

but hushed it open to watch her take the cloth once
more. Watch how her face, legs, feet, wrapped
in wine-soaked shrouds shrank back into obeisance

as she knelt by the altar, unfolded the wings of her sleeves,
and fell to the floor — our Sister crucified: mouth, palms
and belly against the soft new surface of her cross.

THE PALLOR OF SURVIVAL

I'm lucky: autumn is flawless today,
sidewalks freckled rust and red, and the sun
gentle. I'll take the back streets to the bookstore —
it's a longer ride — but I avoid the street where
St. John the Evangelist Church faces that seedy
building with a sign flashing *Jews for Jesus.*
The last time I pedaled between them I felt
a draft there, something so chilling I gasped.

I don't know what happened to Judith
Aaron, placed in 1945 at the Mater Immaculata
convent in Brussels, after she was repatriated
from Bergen-Belsen. Judith who waited eleven
years for some — any — next of kin to claim her.
No one ever came to the black and brass door.

And we never saw her again after
she turned eighteen and left that very morning,
wearing the convent uniform, but the shirt open
three buttons down and the socks low on her thin
ankles. She left on a sleety day in October, years
after — from under a bed in the infirmary —

I'd seen what the nuns did to her when
she confessed she had touched herself: bending her
over, pulling down her panties, thrusting the longest
part of an ivory crucifix between her legs hissing
God Sees You! You'll Burn in Hell!

She didn't let out a sound, not a sigh:
the pallor of survival carved into her face when she

pulled her panties up again. I think she made it:
she was of the stone statues are made from.

And yet, I still search — Judith, I can't
stop searching — for signs we all made it, you, me
and the others, signs I find in the smallest things:
a flawless sky, a leaf autumn turns, an open gate.

DAYS OF RULES

He's like a crow in a crowd of magpies
the old priest who comes for morning Mass
at the monastery. To reach the chapel, he creeps
into the cloister garth by a rusted gate, and slips
through habits dripping on clotheslines: six
identical rows of starched nuns, hanging stiff
and headless by the laundry room rhododendrons.

Inside, bare-armed novices with long
wooden tongs stand around steaming basins,
stirring and fishing out dozens of sanitary napkins.
Each has four loopholed ribbons, fasteners
for the black Bakelite buttons sewn inside
our underpants for *les jours de règles*, the days
of rules. Blessed days: P.E. is forbidden. Cursed
days: washing with warm water is forbidden too:

"*It makes blood flow*," Dorm Sister says,
"*cold coagulates*." So we wash with freezing
water, always wearing our washroom chemises:
rough linen shifts slit on both sides, and tied
on the shoulders with string. No bath, no shower,
we must stand at the sinks, and obey the rule: first
lift the eyes, keeping fixed on the third tile above
the metal mirror and only then the chemise,

We must wash, dry, then put on our underwear
under them, and only then hang the dripping things
on numbered hooks. Anne sometimes disobeys
the rule, lifts her chemise too high, showing us
her shivering body and new breasts: *Je suis belle?*

Sundays, when most of the girls have gone home, Ann and I hide inside the bleach smelling nave of rhododendrons: she coils against me, trembling to be held so close, her cold chapped hands clenching mine, as we watch the old crow mumble his way back through the habit maze, and listen to Bruges hum beyond the stone walls.

THE RADIATOR

Winters in Bruges were a monochrome
  of brown and gray, as were the huge
    wrought iron radiators of the nunnery.

I believed the banging North winds came
  to die in those pipes — I was eight then,
    ugly, awkward and shy.

Nuns slid along granite halls, hands
  in black tunnels of serge. Soon, dawn would cast
    its light through the stained-glass of the chancel.

I longed for that moment, when the hyacinth cape
  of the Virgin bloomed, and the cheeks of Jesus
    blushed as from a sinful dream.

My uniform itched. Knitted socks stopped
  an inch under the knee, flannel skirts
    half an inch above. My thighs

were chapped from rubbing on benches and stiff sheets.
  At 5:45, we stood at the Chapel doors,
    in shivering rows of three.

I was cold, always cold during those interminable
  Catholic winters. Mother Marguerite was late
    that day and the radiator banged next to me.

I lifted my skirt, jumped, and straddled it —
  raw thighs against lukewarm metal.
    Annabelle pointed *I'll tell on you!*

Judith whispered *You'll be punished!*
    The door opened — I froze — like a mad
        magpie, Mother Superior's cornet

flapped in my face: *Get off there!*
    Immediately! she croaked.
        Forgive me, Mother, I dared, *but why?*

Her knotted fingers were ice on my wrist.
    It gives... ideas, she said. I didn't look
        at the virgin's cape that day, or at Jesus blushing:

I couldn't figure out what Mother Superior meant.
    Years later, in the back of a black Peugeot,
        I understood: it was forbidden, hard, warm.

LEEK STREET

in Bruges, was a cul-de-sac so narrow
cars never scarred its mossy cobblestones.
Every house had a niche above the door
for a Saint, and a little garden framed by high
brick walls. Carved into the back rampart,
an iron gate opened on the Wool Canal.
　　　Now and then, a muskrat's head
pearled out of that green velvet, then slipped
back into the water. The Belfry rang a bronze
quiver through the drizzle every quarter.

　　　Yochemke lived at No. 8 in the only house
with open curtains and no Saint.
He was nine, had a large hole in his tongue
and six numbers tattooed on his arm.
They did this to him when he was a baby, he said,
he couldn't remember if it hurt.
　　　I loved him so much I repeated the numbers
inside his arm every night until I fell asleep:
Yochemke-seven-four-three-two-three-six.

　　　It rained the day he said I could put
my finger through his tongue. He shut his gray
eyes, I shut mine, and he slowly closed his lips
around my finger. Something guilty and deep
made me want to cry.
　　　We were setting muskrat traps by the canal
the first time he said he loved me. I wanted
to play the piano for him, or have curly hair and be
beautiful, I was so happy.

The muskrats were for his father
who made collars and hats out of them to sell
at the Fish Market. He always came back
with something for Yochemke.

Once, it was a glass marble with a heart
of green, blue and gold. When Yochemke gave it
to me, we were sitting by the canal stirring the algae
with willow sticks. His father had told him
the heart of the marble was what the world
looked like before the Germans.

That night, we climbed the Belfry tower
to make the bronze bell ring with the marble.
Up there, looking down at the brown roofs
and fields of the world, we wanted to change it back
to how it was, make it look like the marble again.

We'd set traps for the Germans, poke
holes in their tongues, hurl their bodies in the canal,
and all the muskrats would feed on them, and fatten,
and we'd trap them, and —

I'll buy you a piano, said Yochemke, *we'll be
the richest hat makers in Belgium.*

Then, with our marble, we tapped the bell
as hard as we could and listened to its small
sound float out over the canals.

CHANEL N° 5

One by one, my mother dips her *Gauloises Bleues*
    in Chanel N° 5, then puts them to dry on the table,
        on a blue handkerchief laced with flamenco dancers.

Later, she slips each cigarette in a silver case,
    checks her lipstick in the lid, smiles at it,
        and leaves the kitchen, humming to no one.

When the front door slams, I climb the counter
    and through the lace curtains watch her car wink
        left,   *left,*   *left* — and leave.

At dawn, before my parents wake, I run to the garage
    at the far end of the garden, the cold sharp
        and gray like the gravel under my feet.

I open the heavy wooden door: a Dutch bicycle
    hangs from the ceiling, crates of onions, leeks
        and potatoes sprout against dank bricks.

Mother's '52 Fiat is linden green,
    with leather seats, a wooden steering wheel
        and Chanel lipsticks under the radio.

The ashtray is full of crushed *Gauloises Bleues.*
    I lift the bicycle from its hook, slip my hand
        under the mildewed saddle, and find

the matchbox I hide above the springs. A dancing,
    red devil smiles at me from the lid, his horns
        black brackets against a Belgian flag.

I spit in my hands, carefully choose
    the least crooked butt, straighten it by slowly
        rolling it in my palms, up and down,

back and forth, put it between my lips,
    climb on the saddle — and light up.
        When I inhale the *Gauloises Bleues*,

my mother and Chanel N° 5 torch my mouth
    and scald my lungs. I cough, cough, the nicotine
        makes me cry: I can finally cry.

And as I write *Maman* with my *Gauloise*
    in the indifferent air, I dredge up
        the longing for her from my throat — and spit.

ENGLISH FLAVORS

I love to lick English the way I licked the hard
round licorice sticks the Belgian nuns gave me for six
good conduct points on Sundays after mass.

Love it when 'plethora', 'indolence', 'damask',
or my new word: 'lasciviousness,' stain my tongue,
thicken my saliva, sweet as those sticks — black

and slick with every lick it took to make daggers
out of them: sticky spikes I brandished straight up
to the ebony crucifix in the dorm, with the pride

of a child more often punished than praised.
'Amuck,' 'awkward,' or 'knuckles,' have jaw-
breaker flavors; there's honey in 'hunter's moon,'

hot pepper in 'hunk,' and 'mellifluous' has aromas
of almonds and milk. Those tastes of recompense
still bitter-sweet today as I roll, bend and shape

English in my mouth, repeating its syllables
like acts of contrition, then sticking out my new tongue —
flavored and sharp — to the ambiguities of meaning.

LOVING YOU IN FLEMISH

Let me love you in my tongue tonight,
heavy as Percheron hooves on fields
lying fallow and humming with rain,
their rich and dark loam steaming.

I know words lazy as canals
gliding among willows and yews,
green as Memling's velvets
or Bruegel's mossy farm roofs.

Angry clappers on Belfry bronze,
or moaning tugboat sirens, Flemish
undulates like dunes, or glistens
with the spume of granite piers at Ostend.

Taste my language — a salty shrimp —
bitter with chocolate and beer:
the Trappist ale is naughty, the Devil ale
is sweet like cream over sorrel and eels.

I know the lingo of the blue Antwerp alleys
where women lust from the sea — they're
too hungry for one sailor only...
Let me love you with uttered

only there, songs the many-tongued
whores whisper, listen:

> Kom mee oengze nacht in Antwaarpe verdwoale,
> Mokt de klank van de stroaten a' ziel amoureus?
> Al edde gien geld oem plezier te betoale
> 'k zen 'n goe vrake, hiel lief en genereus

Oengder de glans van de moanestroale
Word iel oengze wereld een awelaksbed
Kom mee nor bordiele vol vrawen en matroezen
Verget awe noam en al de rest...

AFTER A NOISY NIGHT

The man I love enters the kitchen
with a groan, he just woke up,
his hair a Rorschach test. A minty
kiss, a hand on my neck, coffee,
two percent milk, microwave.
He collapses on a chair, stunned
with sleep, yawns, groans, complains
about his dry sinuses and crusty nose.

I want to tell him how much he slept,
how well, the cacophony of his snoring
pumping in long wheezes and throttles —
the debacle of rhythm — hours erratic
with staccati of pants and puffs,
crescendos of gulps, chokes, pectoral
sputters and spits.

But the microwave goes *ding!* A short
little *ding* — sharp as a guillotine —
loud enough to stop me from killing
the moment. And during the few
seconds it takes the man I love to open
the microwave, stir, sip and sit there,
staring at his mug, I remember the vows
I made to my pillows, to fate and God:

I'll stop eating licorice, become a blonde,
a lumberjack, a Catholic — anything! —
but bring a man to me.
So I go to him: *Sorry, honey,*
sorry you had such a rough night,
hold his gray head against my heart
and kiss him, kiss him.

PLASTIC BEATITUDE

Our neighbors, the Pazzoti's, live in a long
canary-yellow house with Mrs. Pazzotti's
old father, their 2 daughters, their husbands,
4 kids, a tortoise shell cat and a white poodle.

Their yard is my childhood dream: toys, pails,
balls, bicycles, tubs, bird cages, barbecues,
tools, and garden sculptures: an orange squirrel
eating a nut, Mickey Mouse in a wheelbarrow,
St. Joseph carrying a lantern, his other hand
broken at the wrist, and two toads in an S-shaped
love seat, under a polka-dotted parasol.

On their deck's railing, a procession of nine
pinwheels. They thrash the air like angels
nailed to their posts. At the end of the yard,
two electric cords shoot up to the garage roof.
One connects to a large tennis racket shaped
bug zapper, the other one snakes to, then into
a fake marble pedestal on the cornice.

And there she stands, in plastic beatitude —
and six feet of it — the Madonna, in her white
robe and blue cape, arms outstretched, blessing
the Pazotti's, their yard and neighbors, lit
from within day and night, calling God's insects
to her shining light, before sending those frantic
heretics straight to the zapper.

AUGUST

We are alone again, children and friends
have come and gone, a breath of sage

wafts through the air, I sew a button
to your shirt, it's August — placid, fair.

You're writing in your room,
looking up now and then to stare

at the nasturtium and lavender I
planted by the gate, for their purple

scent, and sedulous reaching. So when
I bring your old frayed shirt to my lips,

cutting the thread with my teeth, I hold
it there simply because it is yours,

and has our smell, familiar and common.
I press the denim against my face, tasting

the air in it, the sun, and realize how
light it is, how easily it could slip out

of my hands, out of this moment —
how the smallest distraction, the slightest

inattention could leave me here alone,
with nothing but my face in my hands.

THE FEATHER AT BREENDONCK

I am praying again, God — pale God —
here, between a white sky and snow, by the larch
I planted last spring, with one branch broken at the elbow.
I pick it up, wave winter away, I do things like that,
call the bluebirds back, throwing yarn and straw
in the meadow, and they do come, so terribly blue,
their strangled *teoo-teoo*

echoing my prayer *Dieu, Dieu* — the same
Dieu who stained the feather I found in the barbed
fields of the Fort Breendonck Concentration Camp
near Antwerp in 1952. My father tried to slap it
out of my hand: *It's filthy.* But I held on to it — I knew
it was an angel's. *They only killed a few Jews here,*
he said, *seven, eight hundred, maybe.*

So I wave their angels away with my feather,
away from my father, away from the icy blue skies
over the Breendonck Canal, where barges loaded bricks
for Antwerp, where my father loaded ships for Rotterdam,
Bremerhaven and Hamburg — as Antwerp grew,
and the port expanded, and his business flourished,
and all the while he kept repeating:

That's all we needed: a good war...

THANKSGIVING INVENTORY

Thanksgiving today. Soaked with sleet.
No sun for six days — six is the Devil's number.
I have looked through this window,
at these American skies for 6 times 6 years.
This is my third garden.

The first two blossomed in Belgium.
Where there is no Thanksgiving.
Where my father is buried.
Where I was raised and raped.
Where I worked.
Where I had five lovers, but loved only one.
Where I gave birth to three children: a son,
a dead daughter, a blond daughter.

Two larches grew in my first garden.
Because of North sea winds, they fused
into one trunk. It wounded them at first,
that rubbing together — the frailest larch
loosing sap for months. A golden sap.
It glued them to each other at last.
I saw it as an omen for my life.

I give thanks for the lowlands in Belgium.
For Flanders, her canals and taciturn skies.
For the tall ships on the river Scheldt.
For coal pyramids in Wallonia.
For the color of hop, and the hop-pickers' songs.
For Antwerp's whores who woo sailors in six
different tongues.

Six is the Devil's number.
My grandfather and a farmer killed six
German soldiers and threw them in a Flemish moor.
I can no longer give thanks for that: I ask mercy.
Before I die, I'll plant a larch by that moor — *miserere* —
I prayed six times for the death of my Jew-hating father,
I ask mercy for that also: it's Thanksgiving today.

I give thanks for my son and daughter,
for the man I love who taught me a new language.
For this garden's trees.
When I left for this vast continent,
I took a leaf from a tree behind Apollinaire's grave.
I took sand from the river Scheldt,
I took an inch of barbed wire from
a Concentration Camp near Antwerp,

but no weed, not a seed of it, growing from my father's ashes.

In Belgium, the day is almost over.
A new millennium already wages merciless wars: *miserere*.
A jacaranda grows in my garden, and two olive trees,
one for my son, one for my daughter —
and far from a moor in Flanders,
I still pray *Miserere*. But for America now. For America.

from
SMALL GODS OF GRIEF

THE RAT TRINITY

That rat's too smart to come to the crumbs
I sowed by the park bench. He has
the patience of true hunger —

he'll wait me out with the same tenacity
I had as a child, hungry to grow strong
enough to escape the nunnery

without being caught. I loved the rats
of Bruges I watched from the dorm window,
how they slunk out

the courtyard sewer grill, slid along walls,
slipped down the cellar steps like whispers,
and vanished into gray.

I loved three in particular. Christened them
the Trinity: the Father was slick, sullen,
the Daughter, tense but lissome,

always kept her eyes lowered, and the fat-
bellied one, the Holy Ghost, maker
of miracles, was the Mother.

I imagined they came from Antwerp,
from the port's stinking sewage by the Cod
Wharf, last quay before the wild, eager sea.

And there were times, when the nuns'
beatings seared my skin with oil hues
on the river Scheldt,

and I squeezed my thumbs in my fists
through long convent nights, there were times
I prayed to the Rat Trinity.

To show me the way out, through Bruges
sewers and cobbled streets, then underground
to Ghent, out again through velvet wheat fields

near Antwerp, and hasten to my parents' house
where Mother wore silk and Father blew
smoke halos in the air.

I prayed the rats to bring me back to the young
whispers of their bed and into Mother's fat,
white belly. To crown them with the trinity

they had hungered for: a Father, Mother,
and from their union not I, but unscorned, welcome
and blessed: one divine being — a son.

FOLLEN STREET

I do it each time we move, do it again
to our new house in this listless Cambridge
street: press my forehead and palms

to the new front door, and say Forgive me,
before I bring in my mess: relics, hopes,
insomnia, clocks.

Then, while the man I love carefully prints
our two names on the mailbox, I chase
emptiness away with broom and books,

hang the paintings, those fake windows
I need to comfort me from what I keep
seeing through lucid ones: the same skies,

traffic, worn-out dogs, and always,
everywhere, an old widow or widower
trying to be dapper —

the woman with dust on her nice little
black hat, and too much blush. The man
in his brown shoes and gray pants, always

too short:. Have you noticed that? It gets
me every time, those inches missing.
And oh, what they carry: his briefcase

so very flat, but something to hold onto;
her bag clasped around her "just-in-cases."
So much like what we bring

to this new house: things. Things to hold
onto, just in case, one day, only one
of our names remained on that mailbox.

G.O.D.'S TRUCKS

I'm not making this up
    — they bolt through
    traffic all year long —
"G.O.D." plastered in black

on their fronts, sides, backs,
    — letters spaced by periods
    big as brake drums —
on rigs roaring all over town, for

Guaranteed Overnight Delivery.

Six- to eighteen-wheelers
    —Volvo engines,
    Bendix brakes —
dispatched across New England's

gritty roads and city grids
    — loading kayaks, anoraks,
    porn, or petunias —
kept track of on G.O.D.'s ledger for:

Overnight Delivery — guaranteed.

Why didn't I think of it before
    — it's been in my face
    all this time for God's sake —
their 800 number the one to call:

no more shrinks, no novenas
    — rosaries clicking

like phones hanging up—
I'll call them for a date with

Guaranteed Overnight Delivery's

roving rep, show him my load
      — how it piles up, weighs,
      chokes up my days—
and sign a contract, swear I'll pay

overtime, taxes, tonnage and tips
      — anything you
      charge, G.O.D. is okay —
I'll pay. But haul it away:

Deliver me. Overnight. Guarantee it.

THE PLEASURES OF HATING

I hate Mozart. Hate him with that healthy
pleasure one feels when exasperation has

crescendoed, when lungs, heart, throat,
and voice explode together: *I hate that!*

There's bliss in this. Rapture. My shrink
tried to disabuse me, convinced I use Amadeus

as a prop: Think further, your father perhaps?
I imagine the shrink with a powdered wig,

pinched lips and mole: a transference, he'd say,
a relapse. So be it, Sigmund. I won't come back.

I hate broccoli, chain saws, patchouli, bra-
clasps that draw dents in your back, roadblocks,

men in black knee-socks, sandals and shorts —
I love hating that. Loathe stickers on tomatoes,

jerky, deconstruction, Nazis, doilies. I delight
in detesting. And love loving so much after that.

HARVARD BRIDGE

This is the day's last offering: the sky bleeds
        like a sacrificial lamb, the sun's wine-bloated
                host slides deep into dusk's throat.

Crimson floods the Charles, banks and reeds blush:
        roofs, cars, puddles and boats are aflame;
                every one, each thing is soaked red —

but no one seems to notice the sun
        drowning in the river like the raised fist
                of a sinking God. I'm in my car, foolishly

trying to make eye-contact with someone: *Isn't this
        amazing?* as cars pass me left and right,
                honking, angry, in a hurry to get

somewhere. What can I do but follow —
        go, brake, blink, bleat with the chorus,
                losing my smile as I join this exodus

toward night, as the sky fades to rust, and stop lights
        flash, and a kid in cap whacks at trash
                cans with his baseball bat.

BENCH IN AIX-EN-PROVENCE

There they are again, the lovers
      — mid-thirties, colorless
    clothes, hair, hands —
having their lunch-break

on the same beige bench
      — in the jabbering street,
     pigeons nodding at their feet —
under a paltry plane tree.

They simply sit there, not saying a word.

For days now, I've watched them
      — from a narrow window
    on the Rue Marceau —
place a single napkin on their knees,

a coffee cup on her side, a beer can on his
      — each at the exact same
    distance from their hips —
and don't drink or eat,

but simply sit there, not saying a word.

There is such resilience in how they sit
      — hands, knees, feet
    together, neatly —
in the way they stare at the pigeons,

or at the clouds moving in like frayed sheets
      — and smile at the same things
      at the same time —
that I know they haven't had it yet, sex.

They simply sit there, not saying a word.

And I find myself hoping
      — as I close the window
      on them, on noon, on Aix —
that they'll wait before spending

their lunch-break having it: sex
      — calling it making love but too soon
      calling it anything but that —
instead of coming back to their bench at noon,

to simply sit there, not saying a word.

OFF-RAMP SWEET BRIAR

A friend betrayed me yesterday.
I loved him for his hungers

and flat feet he stomped as if
he wanted to leave his footprint

everywhere he went. I never
told him how that stomping

moved me, the same sad way
this sweet briar does, waving,

reaching out, trying to be noticed
in the dusty rush of an off-ramp.

My friend betrayed me for a
fast mark, a few gasps around

a spilled secret no bigger than
a briar's thorn.

I'm in one of the cars the ramp
jams into town, and because

it would cause horn-blasting
rage, and because for each

betrayal we lose a little fervor,
I don't step out to pick a leaf

from the briar to keep. To
remember I noticed it.

Lost secrets, lost friends, lost
fervors: we are made of this dust.

Let briars grow from it, and bloom.

DISCOVERING RHYME

They came cheap, the *Petites Punitions* nuns flung
at us for minor sins — dyslexic signs of the cross,
skipped confessions, or whispers during Silence.

Punishments fell: copy two or ten Lord's Prayers
or Hail Marys on calligraphy paper, cursives
correctly curled, capitals clinging to margins:

black ink for consonants, vowels in red. The wars I
waged in those French syllables, wanting the love-
red vowels to win over habit-black consonants!

I hated hailing Mary, for anything full of grace
shamed me: I was homely, eczema chewed
my hands and arms, and had never been baptized:

three reasons for perpetual doom. No Savior's
wine for me, or tastes of His wan flesh on my tongue.
Banished, I spent mass in the back pew,

watching Mary-Magdalene's stained-glass face
as she held Christ's foot in her lap so tenderly.
When it rained, drops flowed down Christ's flank,

and unto her robe — I loved how nothing
distracted her from looking up at Him, how she
let Him quench His gaze into hers.

A winter sun lit that window the day the novices
sang a new hymn. Its melody was rueful, flowed
with long 'ooo' sounds: two words,

amour and *toujours* sung in harmony, over and over —
it was beautiful, I had never heard this as achingly
before: there was music inside the music — words

poured melody into the tune, swooning in unison,
together forever — like Christ and Mary Magdalene.
After that day, I slipped rhymes

in each line of my Petites punitions: Hail *frail* Mary,
blessed art Thou *now* — all my vowels crimson
with *amour*, rhyme my song and music, *pour toujours*.

ON HEARING A HAMMER POUNDING

May 2000

I'm in the garden, pen and notebook in my lap.
Two suns in my tea, the lemon slice the brightest.
Tannin clouds the mug's sky, today's fate still
steeps in its leafy depths. In the distance, a hammer
pounds, and pounds. I count each blow hoping it'll
stops after seven, fourteen, seventeen, twenty-one,
anything with a seven, but it never does. I need
an augury, a sign to help me believe that the pounding
is a good omen.

Antwerp, 1949

My parents are happy hoarding profits
from what they call the good war: a million
hammers, ten million nails are needed

to rebuild Europe, and my father sells
iron and steel. One's misery makes
another's happiness, he says

as we drive through Pelican Street
and what had been the Jewish Quarter.
I am almost seven.

Fifty years later I still remember the winds
blew dust and ashes through the empty bellies
of bombed houses. Some walls still stood.

For no one. Gutted doors and windows
like screaming mouths caught in brick: blocks
of them. And blocks and blocks of them.

Father spits his Chesterfield: *Good! Only*
rats & pigeons left here, instead of Jews.
I don't know that word: *Joden.*

Joden, he says in Dutch. I ask what kind
of animals *Joden* are. My parents look at each
other — and burst out laughing.

(To think I spoke their tongue before I found
mine. O Gods of Grief, grant me this: some
tongues will die, some tongues must.)

Voting Tongue

Yet this Spring of 2000, thirty percent
of the Flemish voted extreme right. In France,
Austria, Germany, Israel, Israel, too —

votes speak menacing tongues and millions
pretend they don't hear it. And I write about
a lemon slice in my tea?

About needing a hammer to stop its blows
in groups of seven because a priest,
from inside a fetid confessional

once hissed to me: "You'll be saved
only if seven generations remember you
as a true Christian"?

Write about Your Times

1961. Oscar Vladislas Milosz teaches writing
workshops in Brussels. I brandish my notebooks
filled with Rimbaud, Aragon, Sartre, Vian, Prévert.

I'm eighteen: *Everything's been said, Monsieur Milosz,*
what is left to write about?
Write about your time, he said, *nothing's been said*
about your time.

Then, on the blackboard he writes: *Le Présent:*
Lieu seul d'où j'écris: Lumière de la Mémoire

(*The Present: Single Place from where I write:*
Memory's Light.)

From which memory must I — will I — speak?
Which present do I — must I — call mine?

Thief, 1950

Oxblood velvet drapes frame Father's office
windows. Ten million hammers pound nails
in Belgium, France, Holland, Italy, England,
and Germany — Germany, too — building
roofs, houses, churches, schools, and bridges
after the war. Father loads iron and steel
onto Antwerp's ships — he's a rich man now.

Home from the nunnery for Easter, I'm
seven. A dusk sun seeps through the drapes,
his mahogany desk gleams a dark blood-red.
I open a drawer, find father's gold *Pelican* pen.
I hear the ships from the harbor urge me:
Doo-it, dooo! — so I reach for it, uncap it,
draw a line in my palm — a strong, hard green.

Summons

Dusk. On my lap, my notebook and pen.
O small Gods of Grief, grant me to write

from seven memories deep, but not in
my father's tongue — but never with his pen.

DINNER AT THE WHO'S WHO

Amid swirling wine and flickers
of silver, guests quote Dante, Brecht,
Kant, and one another.

I wait in the hall after not powdering
my nose, trying to re-compose
that woman who'll

graciously take her place at the table
and won't tell her hosts: I looked
into your bedroom

and closets, smelled your Obsession
and Brut, sat on your bed, imagined
you in those spotless sheets,

looked long into the sad eyes of your son
staring at your walls from a velvet frame,
and I tried to smile at myself

in your mirrors, wondering if you smile
that way too: those resilient little smiles
one smiles at oneself

before facing the day, or another long
night ahead — guests coming for dinner.
So I wait in this hall because there are

nights it's hard not to blurt out: *Enough!*
Stop your Pulitzer, Wall Street, P.C.,
Dante, sex, wars, have some Chianti...

let's stop, let's talk — about our thirsts
and obsessions, our bedrooms and closets,
the brutes in our mirrors, the eyes of our sons.

There is time yet — let's talk: I'm starving.

NEXT TIME

I'll be a cello, rowboat, bench,
snowman, but nothing alive —
no more heft, hope, hunger.

No eyes so shortly fused to the heart
they glut at any goad: TV ads, mall
openings, even "Over the Rainbow"

violining in elevators. I won't be
a gull, whale, snake. No dolphin,
or rat. Not that. I want to be

a thing. Heartless as a parking meter,
tough as a turnstile: a simple, made thing,
An it that knows or fears nothing.

Not even that, at the exact second
of midnight each thing on earth does
live: statues stretch, roads buckle,

meadows sneeze, people in photographs
exchanges stories, and all the carved
initials kiss in their trees.

I can live with that: it's only an instant.
But I'll be a stethoscope. Or willow.
No, better, a mirror, mere reflector:

bare, blunt, facing an opposite wall,
waiting for someone to look for me,
then into me, to check a tooth,

smile, or wrinkle: I'll mirror them
mercilessly. But not for you. Remember
this: find me among the other mirrors,

come stand between that wall and me,
and watch, watch closely: for you I'll lie —
show you only what you hope to see.

FOR MY SON

I sit against the scarred trunk of an oak.
The sun barely winnows through its branches.

Beyond a lit spot small as a newborn's fist,
a twig quivers, then arcs toward light.

What caused such languid inclination
makes its way down the leaf: a tiny snail,

golden in the sun. For an instant, they sway,
lit, in utter balance — then, in a deep bow,

the leaf releases its weight onto earth and curls
back into the shade — the vitreous path

of that moment now in its center. Mathieu,
if nature's cruelties know no limits,

neither do the boundaries of its grace.
I give thanks for you.

FILTHY SAVIOR

Look at this storm, the idiot: it pours
its heart out here, an industrial suburb
of all places, and on a Sunday.

It drenches cinder-blocks and parking lots,
wastes its gusts on smokeless stacks, not even
a trash can to send rumbling down the streets.

And lightning. Forking itself to hit nothing.
What a waste. What if I hadn't been here,
lost too? Four a.m., driving to nowhere again,

a shirt over my nightgown, reciting Aragon
aloud, like an insomniac idiot — scared
to death by my longing for it, death, so early

in the morning, and driving until the longing
runs on empty. The windshield wipers can't
keep up with this deluge,

and I almost run over a flapping white thing
in the middle of the street. I step out.
It's a gull, one leg caught in a red plastic net

snared around its neck. I throw my shirt
over the shrieking thing, take it to the car,
search my bag for anything

to saw at the net, find a file, start sawing.
The gull is huge, filthy, shits and pecks.
I slip a sleeve over its head:

stop it, you idiot, I'm trying to save you —
hold it down, cut, pull, free the leg, neck,
hold the gull against me, fighting for its life,

its crazed heart beats against mine. I step out,
open the shirt — and there it goes, letting
the wind pluck it away, suck it into a cloud

and it's gone — like some vague and bleak
longing — as the rain lifts and the suburbs
emerge in a dirty white light.

AT DAWN

Crows — their constant
beak-clicking, triple-beat squawks.

My love as he sighs, stirs,
weighs a wrist or knee on me,

then sinks back, coiled
into the thick flesh of sleep.

The coffeemaker's chokes,
the garbage truck's brake-squeaks.

Last night's sweet crumbs
of dried-out apricot pie.

Then — light: how it creeps
down night's taut rope, lands,

aslant, on the kitchen counter
to shellac two clementines

shrinking in a chipped bowl.
I take note, write it down: crows' scorn,

love's weight, street sounds —
tastes, colors, death, charms

crammed into a fraction of dawn:
all of this — already gone.

from
A NEW HUNGER

THE RIVER'S MOUTH, THE BOAT,
THE UNDERTOW

Letting go of it — that first balloon — remember?
A dot lost in the air, a voice consoling:
It's just a balloon, you'll get another one.

Too soon you're the one saying: It's only a glove,
dog, lover or job — as you move on, just one of the many
bending over another job, dog, love. But the balloon:
how suddenly it was gone.

How suddenly it was lost. How swiftly hushed
the crying child. How resiliently we adjust
to black dots in the sky: only dust, swallows,

pock marks on the moon. Or planes,
but flying high enough, away enough. Or just
snow, the voice on the radio consoling: only
a blizzard on its way.

A blizzard on its way, and the pain squalls are back
again. She misses him — although what mars
most is no longer the missing, but how

blunt the grief has become. How seeing a man today,
with the same cowlick he had, there, by his left
temple, brought gratitude — and no longer pain.
The heart refusing one more stab of it.

His heart refusing one more stab, had stopped. He was found
leaning against a tree, frozen. His skis a few feet below. Not a red
trace in the snow, just a bruise by his temple, where his head

hit the tree. At the hospital, left alone with him at last,
she lifts the sheet, his gown, takes off her clothes and lies
against him, her face in his neck. She hears nothing. Then,
the wing-whistle of a bird taking flight.

Ah, the wing-whistles of a bird taking flight! No painter
could evoke such sound. No music describe my mother's
glance, at once rising sun and Crow Moon. No clay, wood

or marble render the perfume in my mistress's hair. No
camera could ever capture my oeuvre! But poetry, poetry
does it all... Thus muses the celebrated poet on a bench,
a moleskin notebook in his lap.

In his moleskin notebook, he underlines the word
marvelous. Reads it to himself: "*Marvelous, the odors /*
in my lover's hair." He loves that dactyl: marvelous.

Had it been sung that well before? Wasn't it Baudelaire?
But who, he asks his muse, who'll be the most
immortal of us all? *The clouds,* she whispers in his ear,
over there... over there... the marvelous clouds.

Pierre would quote: *Là-bas... là-bas... les merveilleux nuages...*
while he painted the King's palace gates in Brussels.
She brought him lunch, sat by him on the sidewalk.

They'd sing Jacques Brel together: *Ne me quitte pas...*
May of '61: they were seventeen. Pierre's mother cleaned
the Opera dressing rooms at night. When she left for work,
they ran up to his attic room to make love.

In his attic room, they made love, read Sartre and Aragon.
He'd become a poet, she the next Lotte Lenya. The army
drafted him that fall. Then his letters: *write, please, I miss you.*

She couldn't. Not after what she'd let the doctor do to her —
so he'd take care of her problem for free. All these years
she kept the last picture he sent: awkward in his uniform,
his forehead to the window. The landscape frozen.

A man's forehead to a window. The landscape frozen.
He is old, suddenly. Broken. His last passion, over. Leaving
that woman made it so: he knows this with glacial certainty.

He'll turn to books, crank the stereo in the head-sets,
let it choke his wife's silences and the deafening
cell phone: the other woman calling him, calling still.
Outside, the first snow. Effacing, persistent.

Effacing, a persistent snow. Her husband reads upstairs,
the silence barely broken by his phone's shy chimes —
left unanswered. Over at last, his long nights at work:

the endless meetings, business trips. She hears his study floor
creak — he must be walking to the window again —
she loves how he takes time to day-dream now, and how
he listens to his music, eyes closed, hands joined.

She listens to music, eyes closed, hands joined, headset
lost in thick black curls. A button on her jean jacket reads
Still Against The War. Next to her on the bus,

a small boy frowns, mouthing something to his plastic
police car. Now and then he looks up at an older woman
who has been staring at them for a while. That's
all I'll ever know about them.

All I'll ever know is that we traveled a few blocks together
and nothing happened. What thoughts they had, what
the child mouthed, what music the woman listened to —

insignificant. Right? It was only me thinking the boy wanted
to shoot the class bully from that cop car, right? Or imagining
the older woman was a racist, and the other a dreamer.
What would you have seen? What would you have thought?

What would you have seen? What would you have thought
watching those two men crossing the Brooklyn Bridge, shrill
shirts ballooning, trying to understand each other, hands

swooping up the air like gulls. That the poets gave each other
wisdom or love or even a good time isn't the point — it's that
no one crossing them on the bridge that day recognized them,
or stopped in awe to watch Crane and Lorca walk by.

No one noticed Crane and Lorca walk by, they weren't stars,
presidents, pitchers or popes after all — only two men standing
with empty hands in the murmur of the rivers' mouth.

The two greatest poetic geniuses alive meet, and what
happens? What did they see, what did they talk about,
feel, or think then, as around them the air, clouds and
waters went on shuffling chance and light?

Waters went on shuffling chance and light as the boy
jumped into the river. He had come home from school
that day with a drawing for his dad and found him

overdosed on the couch. The Czech have a word for what
drowned the boy. For what it is that guts a woman's belly
long after an abortion; a word for what hurts, exactly,
when a sheet is pulled over a child, mother, soldier.

In sheets pulled over a child or soldier, there is *litost*.
At the auction of his tractor, *litost* plows a farmer's heart.
In bombs strapped to a terrorist's chest or in the guns

pointed at him — *litost*. Kundera tells us it's untranslatable,
that we have no word for this in English. But here's the point —
what if we did? Would a word make pain more tolerable?
As if language could help.

As if a language could help her survive, the ten-year-old
decides to invent a new one that won't have words for what
she fears, and sees, or for what and who she must forget —

except for brother, mother, and father. Except for that,
she will never speak or understand German again.
She'll make up new words each day, repeat them, learn
them by heart — like songs.

A new language like a song she'll keep singing to herself
the way her parents did on the train that brought them here.
A language without words for hunger, Jew, or Treblinka.

She'll make up a new time also: no hours, nights, winters,
only now and soon, so that when the train will come
to take her back to her brother and parents, it'll be all at once
now *and* soon.

And soon — sure enough — his wife's hand moves
up his thigh to his groin, gently. Fourteen years of this:
her incessant gentleness, and his trying and

failing, failing again to respond to her, or find
a better job, be there for their son, or keep up
with the mortgage — and now her hand
moves away.

She moves away from him, limp with failure,
forearm over his eyes. Would you recognize them
standing in line at the bank, posing in magazines,

smiling at you from home videos? Look: she holds
the cake, he blows the candles and waves at you,
blowing kisses to the past, present and future
of what he fears most.

What he feared most was not death, but to lose wonder.
Death had taught him his first suck, step, words. She
had been his first tango partner, lover, shot of gin;

she coached him on how to stomach longing — she bore
his mother's face, her voice and distance. But it was
on his own, a child still, that he had learned wonder: like
a thief who got away, he stole it from a shore.

He stole it from the sand: a small shell, dull
as the world around him. In the dank stealth of his room
he opened it: the shape of a heart now, it held

the taste of salt on skin, the colors of sails, peach
blossoms in spring. What it no longer held was a void
familiar to him. But what had remained was wonder:
an emptiness beginning to stir.

Daybreak. An emptiness beginning to stir. Less
than a breath, air drafts ripple the water. Cattail
seeds teeter and fall. The color of haze, a crane

lifts from the reeds. Hands in the bib of his overalls,
an old black man stands by the water. Dragonflies
flutter and yaw. A web tugs at a twig —
the man bends to look at it.

He bends toward her, his white-striped spider
in her messy web. He spent hours once, watching her
feast on a caterpillar. He picks a loosestrife leaf,

slips it between his lips, walks away, whistling. Hours later,
the great wrack: trucks, tractors, and a Caterpillar crane
lifting a billboard — *Green Pond Mall Opening Soon!* —
against a blank, tin sky.

In a blank, tin sky — no bird. You, love,
in the footsteps in our house. Or in silences
so unyielding I can hear you swallow.

You and I in the stoop's cracks where weeds grow.
In night's cravings, and beyond them. In our house-
key's clatter, the porch-light's glow. And on bills:
your name and mine in those little windows.

Your name and mine in those windows. Never
in the name we would have given our child.
(Inside the blank, tin sky, love — no bird).

Into again. Into tomorrow. Then, toward the river's
mouth, the boat, the undertow. Within the large
stillness that will follow. Toward that also —
toward the letting go.

STILLBIRTH

On a platform, I heard someone calling your name:
No, Laetitia, no.
It wasn't my train — the doors were closing,
But I rushed in, searching for your face.

But no Laetitia. No.
No one in that car could have been you,
but I rushed in, searching for your face:
no longer an infant. A woman now, blond, thirty two.

No one in that car could have been you.
Laetitia-Marie was the name I had chosen.
No longer an infant. A woman now, blond, thirty two:
I sometimes go months without remembering you.

Laetitia -Marie was the name I had chosen:
I was told not to look. Not to get attached —
I sometimes go months without remembering you.
Some griefs bless us that way, not asking much space.

I was told not to look. Not to get attached.
It wasn't my train — the doors were closing.
Some griefs bless us that way, not asking much space.
On a platform, I heard someone calling your name.

MARCH CHIMES, SNOWMASS, COLORADO

for Maëlle

Day dithers. No wind, quiet birds, still pond.
What's left of the snow a muddy gray.

I step out, tired of all this nothingness. I pick up
a pebble, throw it at the chimes. Their notes

seed the silence, a sparrow chirps in the aspen,
and tiny ripples shiver in the pond.

Every thing around me is waiting for Spring.

And I remember it now, that long emptiness
in me, when nothing stirred, nothing moved,

my body gathering strength from patience,
patience from hope — until that morning

when, both hands on my belly, everything
told me I was pregnant with you.

MY LAST VISIT

The past lies in the swath I left
crossing a summer meadow in Belgium.

I longed to see my old house one
last time, and crossed the field at dawn.

Some weeds lifted their heads
after my passage — purslane and sorrel —

but the touch-me-not lay crushed.
I found nothing there I wanted

to bring back, and no one was there
to see me turn away.

BUS STOP

Sullen, stubborn sleet all day.
Traffic jammed on Sixth. We cram
the shelter, soaked strangers, shivering,
straining to see the bus,

except for a man next to me,
dialing his cellphone. He hunches,
pulls his parka's collar over it, talks
slow and low:

It's daddy, honey. You do? Me too.
Ask mommy if I can come see you now.
Oh, okay. Sunday. Bye. Me too. Bye.

He snaps the phone shut,
holds it to his cheek, staring at nothing.
Dusk stains the sleet, minutes slush by.

When we board the bus, he's still
pressing that phone to his cheek.

GARAGE SALE

I sold her bed for a song.
A song of yearning like an orphan's.
Or the one knives carve into bread.

But the un-broken bread
song too. For the song that a river
sings to the ferryman's oars — with

that dread in it.
For a threadbare tune: garroted,
chest-choked, cheap. A sparrow's,

beggar's, a foghorn's call.
For the kind of song only morning
can slap on love-stained sheets —

that's what I sold my mother's
bed for. The one she died in. Sold it
for a song.

ON A BENCH BY THE HUDSON

Behind me, concrete dumping, steel slamming
and men shouting echo from Ground Zero.

Before me what I come to see, but never do,
that one place in the water where silent, invisible

and drowned, there is a perennial whirl — where
is it? — a swirl in the river where it ends it journey,

takes water and wrecks into the sea. That precise
place (or is it a moment?) that you or I will

never see: a sweet-salted swell made of what is
swallowed, dies, yet flows on, flows into what

it will become — both waters mingled there —
neither river nor sea, but suspended, exquisitely for

an instant. Then, the great ocean.

~~

And his bench I keep coming back to. Where
others also come and go, their presence a whirl

in the air when they leave, before I come
to breathe in the city's swells, watching the Hudson

rush — an ashen estuary — skyscrapers and ships
dragged in its ripples.

Look at me sitting here, speaking softly to

myself in a language that isn't even mine,
staring at a dying river as if I could catch
a truth behind it,

lost in my journey away from my country,
my children facing other seas,

and my pulse a swirl, invisible, drowned —
small beat, rush, sweet salt.

FRIENDS,

this is the viscous heart I hide from you:
gnashing, polluted, hooked to my ribs
like a burr, stuck there and stinging,
and it's only four fourteen in the morning.

Those sudden shudders my waking alarm,
then the daily discipline of shutting away that heart,
shambling through the house, touching things,
stroking their shapes as if it could help me not

be the Bad Sower's daughter each morning:
the pit from a seed he sowed and left to parch,
and no crows would feed on it. So I lived. I don't
want to explain this further, I'm done with it.

But this for you: on the days I touch your books,
read your letters, recall a gaze, the delicate
dangle of an earring, or the throwing
back of a head in laughter,

it's you seeding the first beat into the heart
I open. And as the sun heaves daylight
into the parched tree by my window,
and rats burrow away, when pigeons come

down to feed on dust and pizza crusts, I thrum
the lit syllables of your names on my sill with all
ten fingers, typing them firmly into the brick,
and counting their beats, counting their beats.

NIGHT

Lights go off, one by one, in buildings
across the street. There's something

solemn about this — the lone
drone of cars and cabs

an urban lullaby to shut windows.

Pull the sheet over this day, subway driver,
torah reader, birthday girl, pimp.

Pull the sheet, soldier's mother, corpse
dresser, drunk man's bride.

Sleep my daughter. Sleep my son,

and sleep Jeremiah Smith: the newborn
he delivered in a charity ward today. Sleep.

Wrap a wing around the orphan,
the hungry woman, the caged man.

Shut your eyes, face your walls, the scythe's

blade is tilting toward the earth — so
sleep for the one who knows horror,

or the one who dares speak in any god's name.

Don't listen to the clockmaker: he's setting
the alarm. Sleep until it rings — sleep

toward the waking and the windowless night.

from
THESE MANY ROOMS

ATTIC ROOM IN BELGIUM

Dust covers the window, but light slips through —
it always does — through dust or cracks or under doors.

Every day at dusk, the sun, through branches,
hits a river's bend & sends silver slivers to the walls.

No one's there to see this. No one.
But it dances there anyway, that light,

& when the wind weaves waves into the water
it's as if lit syllables quivered on the bricks.

Then the sun sinks, swallowed by the dark.
In that dark more dust, more dust settles —

sighs over everything. There is no silence there:
something always stirs not far away. Small rags of noise.

Rilke said most people will know only a small corner
of their room. I read this long ago &

still don't know how to understand that word only.
I think of you, love — search for you

in every room that breathes between me & dusk, me & dust.
Love, torn corner from this life.

ROOMS REMEMBERED

[I needed, for months]

I needed, for months after he died, to remember our rooms —
    some lit by the trivial, others ample

with an obscurity that comforted us: it hid our own darkness.
    So for months, duteous, I remembered:

rooms where friends lingered, rooms with our beds,
    with our books, rooms with curtains I sewed

from bright cottons. I remembered tables of laughter,
    a chipped bowl in early light, black

branches by a window, bowing toward night, & those rooms,
    too, in which we came together

to be away from all. & sometimes from ourselves:
    I remembered that, also.

But tonight — as I lean into the doorway to his room
    & stare at dusk settled there —

what I remember best is how, to throw my arms around his neck,
    I needed to stand on the tips of my toes.

[This longing for him]

This longing for him, the choke in my throat again —
               enough, enough.

I throw a coat over my shoulders,
               close the door behind me, softly,

as if afraid to wake another ache.
               Another dawn. It'll seep into the sky

behind the palms. Fists in my pockets, I head east
               into this street

of bungalows as if I belonged here, among the hundred
               windows lit one by one, among the first

joggers & their dogs, past garages yawning out
               cars into the noisy busyness of day.

This longing, again for him, who —
               that June — did not wait for light,

turned his face away from the window &, quietly,
               entered silence.

[I heard]

I heard

how silence swallowed his last breath —

how it followed him

inside the silence after that.

[Arroyo Burro Beach]

Arroyo Burro Beach. The tide dies a while
              then starts its way up again —
                            & up again.

Fog rolls in, dense & sudden. Behind me
            there's a rock halfway to the end
                    of the bay, hunched, split in two,
            black & blue with mussels —

            that's where I turn around & walk
                    back each day. A restlessness
swells inside the tides there — & it's there
                    each time, just before I can look
away — everything
            drowns into itself again & into gray.

I no longer pick up shells — I let them be:
                    waves rake them back & place them
            at my feet again anyway:
small skeletons, empty of life,
                            but pretty.

Look at me, writing circles around what I must face:
            The man I love is dead.

The ashes he asked I lose to this ocean are still
                    in our room, in a red box
            he gave me, for some birthday in New York.

His dust. I'll keep it a while longer — keep it
            as one secretly keeps something
                    for one's self
& won't, today at least,
            lose more of him to these waves.

[Clouds heave]

Clouds heave over the mountains, rip
      & rain — at last. Years of drought,
            yet spring drenches everything
with jasmine stars & citrus blooms.

The hummingbirds are drunk. All night,
         the mockingbird. Each dawn
the call & call of crows.

    Tomorrow, I will have been his widow
for five years.

At first, no tears.
         Everything I was told would happen
as I mourned, didn't.
    No sobs, no rage, no stage
              one, two, three. No
welcome dreams in which he'd appear.

        His cat mourned better than I, lying
on her side for weeks across his room's threshold,
        stretched as much as she could,
           back paws against one side
of the doorjamb, front paws to the other. Waiting for him.

I paced the house, the streets.
             No tears.
I cleaned & sewed & raked & wrote. Sat in the jacaranda's
shade, watched its shadow invade the orchard.

    Walked the beach. Stopped.

Stooped for stones — how they'd huddle in my palm:
    a white one tarred black, the one like a fist,
        & another with a hole bored
            straight through its center.
I threw them back. The metaphors too blatant.

Nights, I'd walk from the kitchen to the orchard
    & measure it, one foot in front of the other,
        head bent, toes to heel, heel to toes,
        whispering numbers.

        Thirty-four feet wide.
        Thirty-three feet deep.

And still not a tear.

[There was a room in Antwerp]

There was a room in Antwerp I loved so much
            I never filled it with books, a bed, or a table.
    It was alive with its own clarity — & I feared
anything left there would etch shadows in that radiance.

The room was in the attic of a hundred-year-old house.
         Hunched under a mansard roof, all its windows
faced the sky. No horizon, no walls, no other windows
            stared into mine.

The wide-planked floor had been painted over for more
      than a century. Scratches in the floor revealed other
          colors under its white surface. A deep scuff
showed a reddish gray, other scratches yellow, green, or black.

       The sun splashed into that room at noon:
cascades of light. Dust, sucked upward by the heat,
    fluttered under the skylight's chicken-wire glass.
I'd stretch out my palms to the rays then,

        & grab that light, lay on my back & listen —
through the whirling air — to the city's guttural chatter,
    the clang of tramway & melancholic calls of tall ships
        with their crowns of shrieking gulls.

I owned that light, alive in my hands.

[So, how are you?]

So, how are you? friends ask, all kindness & concern,
    heads cocked, eyes locked in mine.

&, just like that, I'm his again:
    his wife, his widow: the one whose name

was hyphenated to his — & I'm oddly
    happy to speak about myself,

coupled to him again, finally,
    & say I'm okay, better, but won't say his name

out loud yet because I know
    I'd throw a shadow over the conversation —

all kindness & concern — & over him also,
    who no longer has a shadow.

[The empty room I loved]

The empty room I loved led to a larger one, where I lived.

On the floor, by my bed, askew on a stack of books,
 stood my small transistor radio. It caught
   three stations: One was a pirate radio,
broadcasting from a ship in the North Sea.
  The other, with Flemish news, only came on for two
    hours at night, & the one I listened to most

    was a classical music station.
It played, uninterrupted, for an hour or more,
 then, after a minute or two of absolute silence,
   a woman's exhausted voice came on.
She must have been in her late eighties & constantly
stumbled on musicians' names. I can still hear her
    say "Rack-mun-num-nee-noff."

Every hour, the Cathedral of Our Lady chimed a while —
 then the treble bell rang the hour. I'd stand
   on a chair, lean through a dormer window
to watch how Our Lady's steeple pierced the light.

Summer of '63. I was free, I was twenty. I fell wholly &
 forever in love every week. I was hungry for life

  & satiated by it, reading deep into the night, copying
Sartre, de Beauvoir, Apollinaire, Gide, Rilke, Baudelaire,
   Sédar Senghor, Goethe, Rimbaud, & Lorca
in my notebooks — barely sleeping before I rushed
  down to work, then ran back up
   the five steep flights
    to that white, lit room.

[I was twenty then]

I was twenty then & remember how in stores,
    tramways or cafés, I'd catch someone's gaze,
eyes that took me in &
      held me there
    for an instant. The glint of those stares —
a flash of mica — offered to me &
    just like that, I felt my loneliness
           shatter:
 Everything was light: those eyes & that gaze
holding me — then,
    just as sudden, I
      disappeared again
 inside the dismissal of a blink.

I'd search again & again for other eyes, other heart-
   gasping moments to take me in & hold me —
it didn't matter how briefly
     as long as,
    for an instant, I was
    held.

(And yet, with him, when — from across a crowd, table, or
pillow — his gaze took me in & held & held & held me — it
was I who looked away first. Oh, it was I.)

[Some nights]

    Some nights, settled against him, my face in his neck,
I missed him — feeling that he was elsewhere.
I bought a new bed after he died. His imprint in ours
unbearable — now that he was nowhere.

[Some evenings]

Some evenings, he would hide his face in his hands
            for a few seconds —

then let go of his held breath
                    & lift his head again, his eyes bereaved
of light.

        What room, face, gaze haunted him?

& where you are, friend, in

            Kansas
            Utah
            Rhode Island
            Tennessee —

what haunts you? What is it you choke
inside your palms?

Have you told someone? Have you? Will you?

[I had weeded]

I had weeded, hemmed, counted,
raked, cleaned. I had written
myself reminders: I needed
to wash the curtains. There was
a knot of nettles in my throat,
I couldn't swallow. Swallow,
swallow, I'd say aloud. I was
asleep when he died. I did not
wake when he died. I stood
in his orchard. Heard the wind
stuff night into the tree.
I thought of his clothes. I had
stuffed them in a plastic bag &
vacuumed the air out of it:
I had sucked his air out of his clothes.
I walked to Las Positas Road,
to Peregrina Street, to Pueblo.
From Pueblo up to Stanley,
to Las Positas. I remembered
to wash the curtains.
I remembered to feed the cats.
I was asleep when he died.
I did not wake when he died.
I broke a dish he loved. I had
filled it with water for the birds.
Four years of drought & the birds
were dying — the hills too. No
clouds. California was burning.
I turned the radio off, hearing this.
I squeezed my thumbs in my fists.
I was asleep when he died.

I had to go, I had to leave —
I couldn't remember for where,
I couldn't remember for what.
I drove north on the 101, in the dark,
to Refugio Beach.
I listened to Dylan.
I made a U-turn —
I did not wake when he died.
The mountains are
filled with lost sheep.
I counted the cars I passed
(fifty two, plus seventeen
trucks & a bus.) I drove past
our house to Stella's Café:
he loved to go there
for Happy Hour, he & I
loved to walk there,
he & I, we would —

     & then — there, at last —
     in Stella's Café parking lot,

the tears.

[Horse-hooves, Flemish jabber]

        Horse-hooves, Flemish jabber, & tugboat hoots
ruffle the air. A Sunday in summer. The skylight is open,
    so are the windows. The transistor crackles a piano piece.

I sit in the lit room, by the door, my back to the white
    brick wall — & layer by layer by layer, peel
        away the floor paint in a corner of the threshold.

    Paint petals in my palms. A hundred
years of lives, a hundred keys to this door: a thousand
    kisses under the chicken wire skylight, a century
        of slammed doors, baby's cries.

Women, men, couples moving in, choosing
        a color for the floor. Moving out,
    leaving scuffs & scars behind.

        The color gray was for a stevedore I knew
who read North Sea clouds better than God, but couldn't
read or write.

        The blue for a boy thumbing his marbles
in the grooves between the planks.

Green for the lovers who rushed upstairs, laughing, breathless,
        then walked back down so silently.

But the black paint? The black for the sirens of May 1940.

Hitler's Blitzkrieg blanket-bombing Antwerp —
his Luftwaffe ordered to
              avoid Our Lady by all means:
      Hitler loved her: he wanted her for his Reich.

Then this thin layer — a dusty yellow.

For the Jews.
It can only be for the Jews.

For their yellow armbands under black Stars of David.
For the Jews cattled to the *Breendonck Transit Camp*

sorted, separated,
beat, starved, shot

in *Breendonck*: only 14 miles
away from my white, lit room.

[Dusk at the end]

Dusk at the end of the old stone pier. Pelicans dive
      deep into the waves as we had into each other.

I stand here, remembering that, but can't
      remember his body's weight on mine.

That man I knew by body & skin & belly & heart —
      I have — so soon — forgotten his weight on me.

[Then you stop]

Then, you stop weeping. Lift your face from your hands.
      Not because you're done or because it helped,
            but because there's a faint knock at the window.

You look up. It's a branch. It taps & waves & distracts
      your sorrow. You wipe your face
          hard with both hands.

This is not a sign. You're ruefully aware of that, & don't
      believe in signs. They announced a storm,
          it nears, that's all.

Yet the sky is so still — so lit. Again, those knocks
      at the window. It's not him.
          Of course it's not him.

[For weeks now]

For weeks now, no nettles in my throat.

I clean & count & sew & write & rake.

I walk the ocean's hem & hum a little.

I pick up stones, bring them home:

one tarred black, one with a hole in its center.

I sit by the jacaranda, the stones in my lap.

I'm cold. It's late, the sun turns away,

but just before it sinks behind the hedge,

it wraps a ray around my shoulders, finds

my hands & warms them: weighted,

worn, old, open & lit.

OCEAN ROOMS

The moon trawled the low tide far back behind the beach,
    beyond black rocks, into a shimmer of gravel

& beach glass: a Klimt rug of green, amber, gold,
    hidden most of the year in the ocean's back room.

But it's winter solstice & a large winter sun is all chilled
    radiance this morning. The tourists are gone,

the locals still asleep or on their way to work, so the ocean
    throws open its rooms for me alone, lays bare

a million splinters & shattered deaths: shells & boats
    & glass & bones, letting the sun stun them

with air & light. All of this such wonder & wreckage,
    unburied alive between sky & sea.

I'm glad for this beach, glad for its tides, for things
    that do come back.

Just as I leave — coming close so eagerly —
    a back-lit wave swells, rises, curls, &

drowns this instant back into its kelp-choked rooms.

ROBERT'S KEYS

Silver — a gleam on the corner of Constance & State
yesterday — three keys,
>
> *Robert* printed on a tiny dog tag.

What woman once chose his name as she stroked
her pregnant belly — and who whispers
>
> his name to him today?

I walk, at low tide, along this mussel-gleamed, breeze-
stroked beach. His keys in my hand.
>
> They will never open anything for me.

∴

Because they belonged to others & because I will never
know their story, I pick up
>
> buttons, gloves, ticket stubs —

consoled by owning some small thing from other lives & be
linked to them — as I belong
>
> to their brief glint here, to their dying.

∴

Those keys now against my skin for an instant of impossible
intimacy, no one here to see me:
>
> an old woman who mourns still, paces

a beach, useless keys in fist, as waves open &
>
> lock their large doors as
she hums a small song to herself, almost happy.

SUNDOWNER WIND

Three days now & the sundowner stubborn: a hot hiss
in the jacaranda. It's in bloom. There is no blue
        like this one, dusted by drought & dusk
                        but flowering all it can —

raising its fists to the other blue — up there — sun-fraught,
        contrailed, hazed & exhausted with light, but there,
                        unfailingly there.

The streets are empty, but for a mockingbird on a roof, he too
                doing all he can, singing to the scorched mountains
pockmarked by the Tea Fire.

The sundowner danced
                        with that fire for days,
        its flames still a rage in my old friend's eyes:
        she lost all she had to it.

I think of her often, bent over, sifting
        pottery shards from her house's ashes & finding
                solace there. My god: solace — in so little.

The sun's down. The wind dies in the tree.
        I thumb the two wedding bands on my finger, have them
                do their little dance together: tiny rings
        in a stillness that can't silence everything.

POSTCARD WITH AN AERIAL VIEW OF NEW YORK

Friends,

To think that each of those windows tells
a story in this city's Great Book. A few
paragraphs — not chapters, not pages —
written by us all. He and I met some
of you in those rooms, loved many.
Elbows on wine-freckled linens, we ate
& drank at tables humble & bold.
Feasted, we wrote our own fiction
or tentative truths. Some of you opted
out, or away. Others slipped their names
over yours in doorbell name-holders.
You found us in this city, he & I, writing
our banal, beautiful & forgettable story.
Him & me. Him & me.

ELEGY ON MY DRIVE HOME

for Larry Levis

When it rains on Las Positas Road,
  the trunk of a eucalyptus there turns
 blue — with a few blood-red streaks — but mostly
   blue: a bright
   hard cobalt,

   & it just stands there, bleeding that blue,
among the other eucalyptus trunks in their safe
    camouflage of beige & brown —

& I remember something Larry wrote about Caravaggio,
  how he painted his own face
    in the decapitated head of Goliath,

  & how Larry wanted *to go up to it & close both eyelids*
  because they were *still half-open & it seemed a little obscene*
          to leave them like that.

  I planted a willow in a garden in Belgium when Larry died.
It grew by blue-painted shutters. I wanted that tree
  to keep weeping there after I left for America again —

America who had lost Larry too — & I thought about that,
    & about his two trees, lost somewhere
  in Utah: the *acer negundo*, & the other one
whose name he could never remember.

  So that now, when I drive home I think of those trees:
the *acer negundo*, the other one, & my willow.

Brother limitation races beside me like a shadow too, Larry,
   so that now, when it rains, I take
another way home, or look
      away from the Las Positas eucalyptus
standing there soaked & so
  blue it seems *a little obscene to leave it like that.*

LASSITUDE

It wouldn't take much on a night
like this, to walk into it & wear it,

be cloaked with it, disappear into it,
the stars barely visible above the oil rigs

off the coast, aglow like phantom ships.
Instead, I pick up the old cat who brushes

against the rosemary. She complains
a little: I inhale that perfume in her fur

so wildly. There's a lassitude about her —
she's tired of being the only living thing

in the house with me, tired of how I need
to hold her against me, too tight, too long,

before she can wrest herself out of my arms
& disappear into it — this night.

TWO LONGER POEMS

GREAT GULLET CREEK

Skies over polders are never empty. They return
to brood here, year after year, the old congruent clouds.

There's no better place on earth to be clouds
than over this wild, windblown edge of Flanders:

no place where rain falls hard as willow knots,
dull as North Sea froth, or with that shade of cobblestone gray —

and nowhere do winds whistle this way: peaked and forlorn
like muskrat calls in *De Grote Geule*, Great Gullet Creek.

Once, in a Brueghel winter, a farmer and I sailed across
Great Gullet Creek — on the anger of Flemish winds.

～∞～

Christmas break, 1949. I'm six.
My parents leave me at the *Grote Geule* farm:
they're going on a trip to very-far-away again,
the farmers will take care of me — I must be
obedient, and polite.

One day, the oldest farmer packs
clothes, food, and candles in a large basket.
We'll spend a night in the fisherman's cabin
on the creek: A surprise tomorrow, he says.
All night gales pound at the walls and windows.

When I wake it's still dark. I watch
the farmer light the oil-lamp, dress over his striped
pajamas, pull a small cross from his vest, kiss it,

and put it back. He feeds the stove, throws in
a match and — *whhomp!* —

flames burst out, spiked and golden,
the farmer's face glows, long shadows waltz
on walls, eel-nets swirl, rods and reels wave,
frozen windowpanes glitter, the floor is liquid,
then — *clang!* — he slams the stove shut,

and everything is small and cold again.
We stand by the stove, he helps me cover
my chest and back with sheets of brown
paper we waxed the night before — melting
candles in a tin can, then pouring two layers

on each sheet: Wind-rage armors
he says, handing me blue varnished wooden
shoes. On the table, lit by the oil-lamp,
two twigs of licorice wood, a rock of raw sugar,
an orange, two chunks of black bread.

He cuts the orange in two, shatters
the sugar rock with his knife, and stuffs the pieces
deep into the orange halves. I chew the sour
bread, suck at the sweet fruit. Outside, a cold
light oozes through clouds: daybreak.

~⚬~

Scarves, cowls, coats, gloves. We slip
the licorice twigs in our pockets. Warm
our hands one last time by the stove, open
the door to a wind sharp as nettles.
Door-latch. Gate. Gate-latch.

We walk toward the frozen creek,
he pisses long and steamy on a mooring pole.
Behind the poplars a small sun barely
sifts through clouds. A brown buzzard
cowers in a willow like a quilled Quasimodo.

Flat-bottomed and upside-down,
a rowboat lies in the frozen field. The farmer
slips his hand under the prow, orders Close
your eyes, then Look! Four steel blades dangle
from leather straps: skates! We're going
skating!

We sit on the boat's hull, he
ties the skates to our wooden shoes. The wind
slaps down smoke from the cabin's chimney.
Acrid ribbons of coal fumes tangle with reeds.
From across the creek come broken,

wind-gutted calls of village church
bells, *d-dong… d-dong…* He looks at the sky:
Skating will be good, the wind's angry —
it's coming from Germany. We set foot
on ice, January chews my cheeks,

but I don't utter a sound: he'd
warned me *Only city fillies fuss.* He hunches
like a buzzard before taking flight, grabs
the sides of his coat, opens his arms
wide, turns his back to the wind, lets it

belt against him — propel him:
he orders Crouch, grab my coat,
hold on! A gust whacks me against him,

he takes two wide strides, pulls me along:
the wind pushes us, we're sailing!

The ice is littered with leaves, twigs,
my skates send thunder through my legs,
I can barely breathe. My lips and throat
hurt, but I scream Faster, faster! He straightens
his huge back, opens his arms

even wider, his skates clatter,
pelt my face with ice, we're picking up
speed, the creek sounds like a hundred drums,
my eyes freeze, I can no longer see, but I'm
no city filly, no city filly.

—✧—

When we reach the opposite bank,
our faces are blue, knees so stiff we can't
straighten our legs. I'm thirsty, he gives me
his licorice stick to chew, rubs his palms,

Winter blows low oboe notes
through the reeds. A few yards away,
northern shovelers quack and ruffle
their feathers, sending rust and cobalt
flashes over the ice.

We untie our skates, turn our backs
to the creek, and walk through the potato
polders toward the village of Kieldrecht.
My wooden shoes slip on frozen loam,
I trip, he holds me by the wrist.

The winds won't stop, they churn
clouds, send them crashing into the steel
blade of the horizon. We don't speak,
hurry through the village toward the café
by the windmill.

He pushes open the heavy oak door.
A few nods and taciturn *daag* from stout
drinking men. We head for the high
delft-tiled stove, hang our coats on a chair
beside it. The tables

are covered with thick, ruglike
tapestries, I rub my hands over their wool:
they smell of must and winter, like the hem
of the farmer's coat. He orders Dutch gin,
buttered bread, mugs of broth.

He pours gin in my mug. We slurp
and slurp. He throws back his head, closes
his eyes, crosses his hands on his belly,
smiles. Behind heavy lace curtains, I watch
clouds shred against the church steeple.

~⌇~

On the way back, our skates
ring as he slings them over his shoulder.
Winds blow night deep into the streets
of Kieldrecht. Bundled silhouettes slip
out of low doors, lock shutters,

disappear. Bent figures hurry by
on black, high-handled bicycles: *Good night*

farmer, they say, *Good night farmer*, he answers.
We hurry home through the potato polders.
When we near the farm, the dog yaps,

cows bellow in the barn. At dinner,
I ask the farmer for the cross he hid in his vest.
I kiss it, so it will keep my parents very-far-
away. Outside, the Flemish winds sing.
From the village steeple fall six low notes.

AGAINST AGAIN

The train bursts out of the tunnel into a New Jersey sunset.
A gray haze looms over smoke stacks and storage tanks.

The man next to me reads the paper; he smells of plastic
or glue, and I'm astounded again at those transitory

intimacies we share with strangers: the man's shoulder,
hip and thigh against mine —

even our breaths are in sync —

yet I know nothing of him, and he nothing of me
but my own smell perhaps, which he'll forget even

before stepping off at his station. It will be Rahway —

raw way —

but I don't know that yet.

I don't open the book I hold in my lap: I'm reading faces
around me, a jumble of wonder

and furious exhaustion,

bare, hard features, framed and drafted by birth
toward this commute — since when and to where?—

each face naked with braveness.

Even this small child, harnessed into a dirty stroller:
all she can see are legs. For her,

this train is packed with pants, belts, zippers and shoes —

and look at her face: already courageous, defeated,
and old with it.

~∞~

All I have left of my mother's face is her profile:
the way her face turned away, always —

and how swiftly that profile gave way
to the back of her neck,

and the perfect curls she set there.

For she set them there, each morning,
with willful seduction.

I spent my childhood clinging to an image
of her face bending toward mine.

She was the one kissing me on the lips when,
some nights, I kissed myself in a mirror.

I swear, once, the mirror breathed Chanel N° 5
back into my mouth.

~∞~

The only thing that clung to me was her perfume
the first time she left me at a nunnery. I didn't look at her:

I was staring at my new black shoes — and at two
other pairs of feet: mother's in tan ostrich pumps,
with silk bows and stilettos,

the other caught in thick-soled sandals scarcely
showing under a heavy, dark hem.

When the stilettos
left, I couldn't lift my head.

It wasn't because of the shoes, or the smell of cabbage
smothering mother's perfume,

but because I was turning deaf. Not to Antwerp's
streetcars, or the rain tearing at the windows —

I could no longer hear mother's voice,
yet my suitcase was still

there, on the marble floor.

~

The infant in the stroller whimpers shy vowels.
Her mother flips pages of a magazine. The child

whines again, frets, cranes her neck to see
her mother's face, but the stroller's

black hood is in the way.

The man next to me sighs, uncrosses and crosses
his legs. His hip, for an instant,

away from mine. But then it's back again,
against me. Against again.

And that smell of glue.

～∾～

Nun's faces replaced mother's: thickset in wimples
so tight the wrinkles and jowls were pushed forward

like the skin of wilted fruit — faces without
forehead, ears or necks. Without curls.

I was only four, so that first day, when the nun
carrying my suitcase opened the door

to the dormitory and walked me between
two endless rows of beds, I clung to her hand

and believed her when she said mother
would come back for me soon.

～∾～

That first night: sixty-four new faces, sixty-four
pairs of ravenous eyes stared at me.

Long rows of beds. Cold red brick walls. High
windows. Curtains caught in wrought iron rings.

Sixty-four beds, sixty-six chairs, one between each bed,
plus two extra for a nun at each end of the room.

Then, years of nights.
Years of curtain rings chinking shut.

Murmurs. Whispers. Hushes. The shush
and rustle of small bodies settling into sheets,

the low lament of bed springs, and nights
of silence — faintly alive with the tinkle

of the nun's metal knitting needles
and a new scent that drifted and curled

between our beds like a whisper: the oily,
sharp scent we all shared: Savon de Marseille:

large bricks of green soap Sister Eucharistine
cut into slices with a cheese cutter and distributed

on Mondays. They were to last until Sunday nights.

I learned to wash with water every other day,
so the slivers would last. We all did that.

⁓ꝏ⁓

A girl in one of the end beds — Vivianne —
coughed and wheezed for weeks until we were told

she left for a better place in her Father's garden.

Hannah, to my right, had a harelip
and pinched everyone.

Marieke, to my left cried often,
sucking her pillow's corners:

Marieke and Hannah.
Vivianne.
Sister Brigitte.
Sister Kelleen.
Sister Bénédicte.
Mother Saint-Pierre.
Mother Superior.

My mother
gone.

And in storage, my suitcase.
Inside it, my name bracelet and stuffed dog.

On the dormitory chairs, our uniforms
neatly folded. Nothing else. We couldn't
own anything from home.

But the chairs, the high-backed oak chairs
were ours, labeled with our names in black cursive.

—◦—

Who knows what became of the other chair, the one my mother
flung, years later, missing me at first — down on my knees,
arms over my head — but she hurled it again. It hit my neck.

I had spilled ink on her rug.

She was beautiful, violently beautiful and blonde.

Her laughter — a child's — sprinkled the rooms
with prettiness, the way sparkles skittered on walls
when her rings caught the sun.

Someone had died in the family that week.
A taxi drove me home.

Father smelled of Cologne. He smoked
Chesterfields from a golden holder.
Ashes fluttered like tiny moths on his lapels.

Mother wore a Brussels lace veil and elbow-
length gloves closed by long rows of tiny black
pearls like glimmering rosaries.

She dressed me in a blue velvet coat, with black fur
pompoms as buttons, urging me to be polite:

Say thank you if someone speaks to you.

At the funeral, she whispered how adoringly
the priest's alb had been embroidered,
how delicately refined it was —

and hours later, I had spilled ink on her rug.
Ink!

⁓Ↄ⭘⁓

And it comes back to me: how adoringly I'd breathe —
in sync with her —

the few times she held me. Soothed, sated by her
perfume, my face in the curls she poised on her neck,

I felt chosen — possessed almost — by un-brokenness.
Not peace or consolation. Un-brokenness.

And for weeks I existed, almost whole, after
she dropped me off at the convent again.

I waited for a letter, card, or call. Months of waiting.

I still have the handkerchiefs she gave me, seven
of them, each embroidered with the name of a day:

Lundi, Mardi, Mercredi...

The nuns allowed me to keep them: handkerchiefs
were useful. They *served*.

―∞―

Years of days, also. Matins' incense
escaping into sun-rays.

Boiled fish and rutabaga. Stewed horsemeat.

Boiled beets we'd rub on our lips and cheeks
like make-up, and were punished for it.

―∞―

Beatings and punishments: closed-fist
punches to the back of our heads:
they didn't leave bruises.

Kicks in the back of the knees until they buckled.
Gravel in our palms, scrapes on our legs
that Sister Cecilia dabbed with Mercurochrome.

―∞―

And silences.

Silence in the refectory, silence in the halls,
at mass, at wash-sinks, in study hall.

Silences so long I coughed to break them.

Winters so sunless I prayed to the moon to warm us.

Months between postcards from Baden-Baden,
Florence, Amsterdam or Shanghai,

with only Father's four, spiked, green-inked letters
"Papa" under her blue "Maman" —

that blue ink I had spilled on her rug.

⁓ও⁓

And springs — bright with Easter colors. Golden,
waxed refectory tables, honey-colored wicker baskets

brimming with eggs we painted for prisoners
and the poor.

Knitting and embroidery classes. Years of knitting
socks for prisoners and the poor.

Gray with black borders. Black with gray.

And Kristien, some nights, who slipped into my bed
to hold me, pressing my palms against her face,

kissing them as I kissed the back of her soap-smelling
hands — calling them *Maman*.

Then in June the linden tree bloomed, the air
fervent with its perfume.

We helped novices stretch sheets under the tree,
and, hanging from them, shook its limbs, giggling
as we harvested pillows of gold and green:

a smell so sweet the breeze — drunk with it —
strewed sunlight, bees and leaves all around us.

Sunday nights, we drank the linden tea, its soothing,
blond aroma curling in my mouth.

Stations have come and gone. The man next to me
sleeps. One hand on his thigh, the other on his paper,

palm up. His fingers twitch faintly, and I suddenly
long for that hand, yet just as suddenly need it to turn

palm down on his knee, and stop being so intimately

open there, vulnerable and foreign.

I'm sick of this train, the fleeting faces, the man's
frayed sleeve

and unavailable body half fused to mine,
its smell fading away — it too turning away

from the choked chaos I'm made of, the vortex
I come from — odors, profiles, chairs, soap,

kisses, hands, schedules and stations
swept into the past, lost among smoke

stacks, storage tanks and all those trains.
All that wandering.

—♾—

The train slows again. The man stirs,
rubs his face and neck with both hands,

stands, folds his paper neatly,
and leaves it on the seat.

I don't move, don't dare look up and sit
there, staring at my shoes as I feel him

disappear — my whole body feels him leave.

—♾—

That was it.

A transitory nearness,
a transit story.

And always this hunger,
an exhausted longing —

the wait and the weight.

NOTES

Page 18, in "Early Morning Considerations After a Night of Rain":

"Sempiternal" is from the Latin word "sempiternus" is an archaic English word denoting the concept of everlasting time, that can never actually come to pass (a concatenation of the root "semper" and the suffix "aeternum"

Page 31, in "Little Sisters of Love and Misery":

"Pie Jesu, tantus labor non sit cassus" is Latin for "Jesus blessed, let not in vain such labor be."

Page 47, in "Loving You in Flemish":

The Flemish verses are a loose adaptation from a song by Wannes van de Velde.

> Let's lose our night together in Antwerp,
> Don't the sounds of the street seduce your soul?
> And though you're too broke to pay for pleasure,
> I'm a good little woman, real cute and generous.
>
> Under the glimmering rays of the moon
> The whole world will be our honeymoon bed
> Come with me to brothels full of women and sailors,
> Forget your name and all the rest...

Page 53, in "Thanksgiving Inventory":
"Miserere" is a prayer in which mercy is petitioned.

Page 137, in "Great Gullet Creek":

A *polder* is a low-lying field created by dikes. The polders in this poem, between the sea and the river Scheldt, were drained to cultivate potatoes and leeks.

ACKNOWLEDGEMENTS

My grateful acknowledgment to the editors of the following publications in which these poems, some in different versions, first appeared: *Anacapa Review, Askew, Cavewall, Crosswinds, Five Points, Gyroscope Review, Hush Review, Lily Review, Miramar, Orion, Pedestal, Plume, Poem-a-Day from the Academy of American Poets, Salt, Santa Barbara Literary Review, Solo, South Florida Poetry Journal.*

Such glad, sincere & cheering gratitude to VOX POPULI & Michael Simms, not only for generously publishing my work, but also for the awe-inspiring and selfless work you do to support contemporary poets, essayists & non-fiction writers. We owe you, friend.

Thank you to BOA Editions & Four Way Books (merci ma Martha!) for having been such solid & generous supporters of my work.

"Evening" is for Susie Read Cronin.
"Late Afternoon Stroll on the Cliffs" is for John Murillo.
"Provenance" is for Mathieu, Sara, Tibo, Maëlle & Jeff.
"Complaint About Missing Friends A Year Into the Pandemic" is for the poets Gudrun Bortman, Mary Brown, David Starkey, George Yatchisin & Chryss Yost — thank you for your mighty helpful edits & joy-filled Sunday afternoons.

To my sewing circle — my thanks for the yards & yards of laughter & friendship.

Thank you to my students who continue to delight & inspire me — & in memory of my teachers Kurt Brown, Brigit Pegeen Kelly, Larry Levis, Thomas Lux: how I miss you.

My gratitude for you, steadfast friends, for your hearts, trust, and your listening: Aidan O'Brien, Nickole Brown, Chris Buckley, Susie Read Cronin, Steve Huff & Betsy Gilbert, Jessica Jacobs, Meg Kearney, Christine Kravetz, Marsha de la O, Martha Rhodes,

Marieke Ruefle, Tim Seibles & Jennifer Fish, Michael Simms, Phil Taggart, Brian Turner, Jace Turner, & Yoenemoenneke.

To Chryss Yost & Sungold Press: what joy, ease & elating experience it was to work with you on this book.

Mathieu, Sara & Tibo; Maëlle & Jeff: right here, dans mon coeur.

Sempiternal love, Kurt Brown — and in memory of you — patient, tender, intent & witty companion & accomplice.
I'll catch you later down the road, love.

Laure-Anne Bosselaar is the author four previous volumes of poetry including *The Hour Between Dog and Wolf* and *Small Gods of Grief*, which was awarded the Isabella Gardner Prize for Poetry. Her third poetry collection, *A New Hunger*, was selected as an ALA Notable Book. Her most recent collection, *These Many Rooms*, was published in 2019.

Her poems have been widely anthologized and have been featured four times on Garrison Keillor's *The Writer's Almanac*. She is the recipient of a Pushcart Prize as well as the James Dickey Prize for Poetry. She is the editor of multiple anthologies: *Night Out: Poems about Hotels, Motels, Restaurants and Bars*; *Outsiders: Poems about Rebels, Exiles and Renegades*; *Urban Nature: Poems about Wildlife in the Cities*; *Never Before: Poems About First Experiences*; and *While You Wait: a Collection by Santa Barbara County Poets*.

Bosselaar taught at Emerson College in Boston and at Sarah Lawrence College in New York, and is a member of the founding faculty at the Low Residency MFA Program at Lasell University. She taught at the College for Creative Studies University of California Santa-Barbara, and served as Santa Barbara's Poet Laureate from 2019 to 2021.

www.ingramcontent.com/pod-product-compliance
Lightning Source LLC
Chambersburg PA
CBHW020256130626
46549CB00005B/2239